To Shauna
with every good w...
love & gratitude
Brid

THE MYSTERY OF THE SENSITIVE CHILD

Bríd O'Donoghue

First published in the Republic of Ireland 2023
Copyright © Bríd O'Donoghue 2023
Bríd O'Donoghue has asserted her right
under the Copyright, Designs and Patents Act, 1988
To be identified as author of this work.

ISBN 978-1-7393163-0-3

Cover design by Niamh Faherty.
Editing by Maria Lockett.
Formatting by Caroline Kenny Redmond at Kennys Bookbindery.

Printed and bound in the Republic of Ireland.

ACKNOWLEDGEMENTS

My sincere thanks to all those who took the time
to write and share their personal experiences.
These stories form an integral part of the book
and help the reader gain a deeper understanding of
the challenges faced by sensitive children.

Also, a word of thanks to my friends who helped
transform my transcript into this book.
Maureen for providing a space to assist me in putting
my thoughts in order,
Bernie and Mary for all your input and attention to
detail.

Go raibh míle maith agaibh.

DEDICATION

For much of my life I felt different, as if I was a silent observer to the lives of others. Often misunderstood and unable to explain my challenges and my sadness. In more recent years I have met many sensitive and empathic people. We are not the odd ones out. There are millions of us whose daily lives are impacted by our environment. This book is dedicated to all those who find themselves challenged by their levels of sensitivity.

CONTENTS

INTRODUCTION

The sensitive child is exactly that, a child who is sensitive to their surroundings. Every day they sense the feelings of those around them. In their home situation, they will become accustomed to their family members' having various temperaments and personalities. Everyone learns to adapt to their environment, but for these children there are extra challenges. They literally absorb the emotional states of those with whom they share spaces.

The word Sensitive, in its truest form is: *"Someone who senses other people's needs, problems, feelings or pain and shows compassion for what the other person is going through"*.

Most people will feel compassion. The sensitive child takes this to a completely different level. They are literally sensing the needs, problems, feelings and sometimes the physical pains of other people. Even if the other person is hiding their distress, the sensitive child is still aware of it. The stronger the emotion being experienced by others the stronger the impact on the sensitive child.

As they grow and absorb copies of the personalities within the family unit, they will develop techniques to adjust and cope. But then, at the age of four or five, they enter the educational system. For some children this happens at a younger age if they attend crèche or childcare. They go from experiencing the energy of their family unit, to experiencing the energy of an entire classroom. They are now totally bombarded as they absorb the emotions of all the students, teachers, teaching assistants etc. This happens against a backdrop of the child having little or no understanding that the feelings they experience are not their feelings at all. They can spend most of their childhood overwhelmed as if continuously walking a tightrope and never knowing when they are going to lose their balance. With each simple interaction they risk absorbing new emotions and this will change how they themselves are feeling and behaving without any understanding or explanation.

This all combines to add to the mystery surrounding sensitivity. Why do these children present with so many varying behavioural responses?

- Withdrawn, anxious and struggling to participate in life.

- Impacted by their environment and the feelings of others.
- Behaving as people-pleasers and problem solvers.
- Some will hit, kick, or bite without apparent provocation.
- Feeling pressure on their chest and having stomach pain.
- Feeling distressed and crying more than their peers.
- Demonstrating a high level of compassion for the needs of others.

Irrespective of their level of sensitivity, every child will face their own challenges as they negotiate their way through school. Each child has their own label, e.g., dyslexia, dyspraxia, anxiety, physical disability, there's an endless list. The educational system globally has made tremendous strides in finding ways to support and assist children with these labels. But not so for the sensitive child. For these children to thrive in the educational system, there is an even greater need for openness, understanding, practical strategies and coping tools.

In my endeavours to bring clarity to this subject, I have given examples from my own life. Some children, their parents, therapists and teachers have also graciously sent me their detailed stories to include. This may assist the reader to come to a better understanding of how being sensitive can impact children, both positively and negatively. As some of the stories and examples are of a very personal nature I have, on occasion, changed names and some specific details to protect their identity. These children have motivated and inspired me to be their champion. My words are spoken as a voice for those previously unseen and misunderstood. These children hold the key to unlocking The Mystery of the Sensitive Child.

Thankfully, strides are being taken to make education and society in generally all-inclusive and to embrace the individual. Conversations are being had in primary schools on topics which would have been seen as 'taboo' for previous generations. This is an evolving knowledge with much yet to learn but we are ready to commence the journey. Finally, the sensitive child is beginning to be noticed, in their own right, with their own challenges and abilities. How wonderful it will be when all those tasked with the care of these children gain a better understanding of what it truly means to be sensitive. To compassionately assist them in their challenging lives as they come off the tightrope of balancing their needs with the needs of those around them. It is time to solve the mystery.

BEING SENSITIVE

The word sensitive is often seen as a negative:

- *"Oh, they are always crying".*
- *"I can't get a word out of them".*
- *"Cry baby".*
- *"Unpredictable".*
- *"Withdrawn".*
- *"They keep getting involved when it has nothing to do with them".*
- *"They are up one minute and down the next".*

The more sensitive or sensory a child is, the greater the differences they will notice between themselves and others. The sensitive child may try to hide their sensitivity so that others do not treat them differently. Every child wants to fit in and to be part of the group; to be included in daily activities. To be of value and not be seen as if there is something odd about their behaviour, simply because their emotional response is often different to that of the majority. No one wants to be seen as the weak link. Well intentioned parents, coaches, caregivers etc. may advise them to *"toughen up"* hoping this will help them to blend in with the *'norm'* or not be a target for bullying. However, we cannot change our genetics to blend in, no matter how hard we try. If a child is sensitive to their environment, then they are simply that.

People can be slow to own the label *'sensitive'*. It has, for so long, been perceived as a weakness. Society, in general, lacks an appreciation of how incredibly difficult it can be for a person who is open to the feelings of others as well as to their own pain. If one is sensitive, then it is an integral part of who they are. When society understands the true meaning of this word, with its challenges and implications, then people may be open to learning ways to reduce the impact. For the sensitive child, only then will it be easier to accept this label and start to see sensitivity as a positive quality.

For adults to assist sensitive children with their life difficulties, they must first come to an understanding of the actual challenges faced by the child. The analogy I use is that of a builder's spirit level. When the level is placed on a flat surface; most peoples' sensitivity is positioned in the bubble in the middle. Those in this bubble will see someone smiling and think, that person is happy. If they see someone crying, or with a sad demeanour, they will be sympathetic to that person. If a person has been injured, they will offer them

6

care and assistance. If someone is aggressive or abusive, those in the bubble will notice this behaviour. They observe people's facial expression, body language and demeanour and respond accordingly.

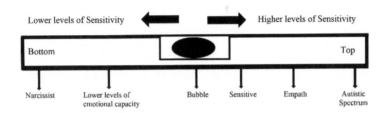

Returning to the example of the builder's level, we now start to move away from those in the bubble in the centre. The various positions on the level represent the person's degree of sensitivity. The higher up the level we go, the more sensitive, the lower we go the less emotional sensitivity. Halfway between the centre and the top of the level, we reach empathy. An empath being: *'Someone who has an unusually strong ability to feel the mental and/or emotional state of another individual'.*

Continuing up the level past empath we travel into the autistic spectrum. Here we encounter varying degrees of sensory overload, making it even more challenging to participate in society.

Below the bubble, represents those with less and less emotional capacity. These people, for varying reasons are frequently not emotionally present. At the very bottom of the level, we come to those who appear completely void of emotional capacity. These people are generally considered narcissists. The narcissist being described as: *"A person who is overly self-involved and has an excessive interest in or admiration of themselves".*

Society recognises that there are narcissists, people with little or no compassion for others. Equally, it is accepted that people can have narcissistic traits, but are still capable of some level of compassion. It is also acknowledged, that those on the autistic spectrum are in sensory overload. Between those in the bubble, who form the majority of everyday humanity, and those at the very top, whose senses are overloaded, exist those struggling with varying degrees of sensitivity.

SWITCHING OFF

I grew up on a small dairy farm in the West of Ireland, an idyllic childhood in many ways. I now understand why my seemingly idyllic childhood proved so challenging for me. Back then I had no knowledge or understanding of what it meant to be sensitive.

My education was '*at the hands*' of the Sisters of Mercy. I have often reflected on the irony of the name of this religious order, as my experience was the opposite to mercy. With hindsight, I realise my sensitivity is at a different level to most other people. For no apparent reason, I was frequently overwhelmed; felt pressure in my chest, had an upset tummy, was emotional, felt a sense of injustice, was near to, or, in tears. Added to this sensitivity is the fact that I am dyslexic, resulting in daily beatings from these Sisters of Mercy.

Now, with that same hindsight, I realise those tasked with my education were not just '*in the dark*' when it came to working with children with varying levels of sensitivity. They were also completely lacking in an understanding of the range of learning difficulties.

They had no logical explanation for my apparent lack of academic ability. Thankfully dyslexia, like many other difficulties, is now a challenge which is addressed with understanding. Teachers are trained to identify the signs of dyslexia. Tools are put in place to assist the student overcome the problems presented by such learning difficulties. These children are helped to learn on an equal footing with other students. Unfortunately, this is still not the case for the sensitive student.

As school was so difficult for me, I developed my own tool, or coping technique. I learned how to step out. Not physically, unfortunately; I would have truly loved to have been allowed to physically step out of the room, the building and the entire school complex. I learnt how to switch off my emotions. First and second class (age six to seven) were particularly difficult as I received daily punishments for spelling errors. Looking back, through my adult eyes, I now place that nun on the lower side of the builder's spirit level, void of compassion. Her method of teaching was literally to beat the child until they got the right answer. Even at six I knew this method was flawed. If I didn't know the answer before she hit me; I was no more enlightened afterwards. To avoid hurting her hands while *'encouraging us to the right result'* she used a piece of wood. This had originally been the arm rest from a wooden chair. It was about a foot long and perhaps an inch deep. It hurt. For any adult to ask a six-year-old to hold out their soft little hand to receive a smack from this device; they could not possibly have any emotional connection with their fellow human.

I developed my own technique to survive the physical and emotional pain. I learned how to turn off my emotions, I switched off my feelings. It was as if I became a robot. I functioned, attempting to do my class work as instructed. I couldn't cope with all the fear. I now understand much of my fear and feelings of injustice also belonged to the other students. I simply shut down. Every time I had to walk to the front of the room to be slapped for an incorrect answer, I functioned robotically. The teacher was left looking at a blank expression on my face, devoid of emotion, which I now realise must have annoyed her even further.

My coping skill served its purpose, as without it I would have been completely overwhelmed. Switching off meant I didn't have to acknowledge the pain. I describe it as being similar to putting all your feelings, your heart and even your soul, into a balloon. The balloon floated beside me attached by a ribbon. When I was safely back at home, I could allow the balloon back inside.

For those using this technique, it comes at a high cost. Our emotional development can be delayed. The longer we stay detached, our emotional development falls further behind our peers. We can also struggle with making real friendships. As a young adult living in London, where it was safe to be emotionally present, I felt immature compared to my peers. When faced with any challenging events or criticism at work (even positively reinforced criticism) I reverted to my old technique of switching off my emotions. This meant small issues did not get talked out. I didn't express my opinion. I wasn't emotionally available for these conversations. I had switched sides on the builder's spirit level. Instead of being near the top of the level, that of highly sensitive, I moved to the lower side of the level. I was no longer sympathetic to those whose space I shared and who were simply expressing a different viewpoint. This must have been very confusing for my friends and work colleagues. As I alternated between being caring, understanding, encouraging and gentle - to non-emotive and detached.

I have met many sensitive people who, like me, switch off in public. Then switch back on when with family or those with whom they feel safe. In normal development, children learn as they grow, to balance and regulate their feelings and any emotional pain. While in school I expected to feel terrified and overwhelmed. Therefore, I used my safety control of switching off. However, in other settings, at home, visiting friends or attending functions where I had felt safe, I was emotionally present.

Life is not predictable. Even though I was familiar with those around me and the daily routines, life did not always run to schedule. People can get sad or disappointed, concerned or fatigued or even become ill without warning. An unexpected guest can arrive at the door. A phone call can change our world forever. News headlines can introduce different emotions. TV and radio programmes can change the feelings of its listeners simply by playing various types of music or reporting on world events. In rural Ireland we have local radio stations. Every day the local deaths are announced with details of the funeral arrangements. These announcements can include unexpected headlines which impact those listening. Although we all live in our own local communities, through technology we have become a more global community. Because I was generally switched on emotionally in my home environment, I could easily change personality and behaviour to match those in my company, or those I had connected with through technology.

We will all have seen young children extremely distressed over minor events. They are learning how to experience emotional distress and how to express it. Their caregiver will offer sympathy and comfort. In a healthy environment the child learns how to adjust to differing levels of pain. They learn their body's pain threshold both physically and emotionally. They learn how to respond to challenging situations and how to regulate their emotions.

In a safe environment, when a sensitive person is switched on, there may be an unexpected event, a crisis, or an unexpected danger - the resulting emotional pain is unexpected, and this pain may be very difficult, or impossible to process. Given that so much time was spent in switched off mode, their emotional development is likely to be hindered. Others will assume the sensitive person is operating on an emotionally similar plane and will not understand the sensitive person's response. Those who are switched on intermittently are at a disadvantage to their peers, as the regulation of the emotional response may be underdeveloped. Ironically, those with heightened emotional sensitivity can be emotionally immature!

Sensitive children will know when they are safe and loved and thus remain open. They are familiar with the feelings of their family members on a day-to-day basis and generally are not overwhelmed in that setting. Whereas for others it may be the opposite. Some may feel safe in a school setting but not at home with their family. Those using this tool, are switching on and off depending on their environment.

The longer that one uses this technique the more of life one misses out on. It's not just difficult conversations that are avoided. Switching off becomes a normal way of being. It's not daydreaming, its simply not being emotionally present. Large chunks of time can just vanish. Those switching off, are functioning robotically and safely. It becomes a way of life, a way of being. But it is not an effective coping mechanism.

I now actively remind myself that *"it is safe to be present, safe to hear what others have to say"*. I now have safe boundaries, can express my own opinion and want to hear what my family, friends and clients have to say. I want to hear their positive and negative comments. If they have a problem with something I am doing, I realise **they** have a problem. I have triggered their emotional baggage and - as these are people I care about I want to avoid adding to their baggage. I need to be emotionally present to hear them.

Those who use switching off as their coping tool are missing out on so much of life. If all the missed moments were added up it would probably add up to years, not days. Our time here is precious. We want to live every minute. If we are not emotionally available when a loved one is explaining their point of view - this will lead to problems. The other person will likely think we don't care how they feel; and/or don't value their opinion. If we are doing something that upsets them, chances are it is triggering something from their childhood. Perhaps they just need our help and understanding. Having voiced their upset, it will be so much better for our friendship if we can hear them and process their truth. Our relationships can finally grow in a healthy way. It may not be pleasant to hear their emotional pain, but if we want to have healthy relationships in our lives, we need to be present. Alternatively, they will realise we are not really hearing them. They may feel we don't care about their situation or opinion. For healthy friendships to develop both parties need to feel valued and appreciated, not ignored.

Now, to ensure I stay switched on, when I find myself drifting, I take two breaths. As the first breath fills my lungs, I tell myself that *"it is safe to be present"*. With the second breath, I imagine it going all the way down to my feet and I tell myself that *"it is safe to be in my body"*.

The human mind is very clever and has developed ways of securely storing away the memory of traumatic events. It may be years before the mind starts to bring flashes of these memories backs. This coping mechanism is meant for occasions that are too difficult to acknowledge at the time. Usually these are one-off events, or there may have been repeated incidents of abuse or trauma that were blocked out. Years later, when safe to do so, pieces of memories from those events may start to re-emerge in our awareness. Perhaps a smell or a taste will trigger the memories. This technique of blocking out memory is not meant for everyday life. It is the body's way of coping under horrific conditions. Unfortunately, for many sensitive children this technique is used daily.

I was one of the fortunate ones in that I had a safe place. For me that place was on our farm. I knew I was loved and would be provided for. There were clear rules on acceptable behaviour and on our individual responsibilities. I understood the rules. I understood the character of my family members. No matter how bad the school day was, I knew I was going home at three o'clock. I could escape the injustice and abuse. I could switch back on. However, for some children home does not offer a safe place. For these children, who desperately want the love and approval of their families, when they do switch on, all they receive is physical and/or emotional pain. They will sense the undercurrents in the house and want to '*fix*' everything. Unfortunately, these situations are generally beyond the limits of a child's efforts. When our family members do not understand our pain, or worse are the cause of our pain, there is no safe place.

Crying Little Girl
NORA

I went to see Bríd in Summer 2022. I didn't know why I made the appointment. I didn't have a particular reason to. I had no health issues, but a friend had mentioned she'd helped her greatly during a time of need, and I was drawn to contact her. I was at a crossroads in my life and knew I had to make changes but felt frozen in fear. I felt something was holding me back, something deep in my childhood. I wanted to move forward but felt stuck. I had no idea what I was going to say to Bríd, but felt instantly comfortable, surprising myself as I opened up.

I told her of my memories of childhood, my memories of being a little girl, sitting in a kitchen, crying, being mocked by both of my parents. As a helpless child I sat there powerless, night after night, unable to open my mouth, like a rabbit in the headlights of a car. "*Why are you crying?*" my mother would laugh, rolling her eyes. My father would chuckle along, making drunken passes at his wife. I never

18

replied, as silent tears poured down my face. I felt no connection with these people, or my siblings. I was the only child who had to sit in this kitchen nightly, crying. I didn't know how not to.

When I committed a minor misdemeanour I'd have no voice, unable to offer the slightest argument in my defence. A chronic bed-wetter, I was reminded nightly that the doctor had said my problem was down to laziness; it was time to cop myself on. When the humiliation ended, I would be sent to bed; where I would lie awake miserable, crying, biting my nails to the quick, afraid to go to sleep, to wake to the inevitable sodden mattress. No matter how many times I went to the loo. Listening to the raised voices downstairs I would torture myself. Sometimes I would sneak back down to listen at the keyhole, to the ongoing assassination of my character.

Bríd suggested my parents' appalling behaviour towards me was mainly due to ignorance and their inability to recognise a sensitive child. This resulted in me leaving the scene (in my mind), building a wall around myself, presenting a false bravado to the world. I continued to be bullied and easily hurt, never having learnt to stand up for myself. Never having allowed myself to be valued, a basic human right. I eventually protected myself by adapting a complete indifference to the whole family, distancing myself in every way I could.

Bríd asked me to visualise taking that little girl's hand and giving her a big hug, assuring her she was loved, that she was safe, and that nobody would ever laugh at her again. I told my Child Self what had happened in the past was not our fault. That it was over, that it was time to move forward, to stop looking back. Bríd sent healing to myself, the damaged little girl, and my parents. She guided me to think about my future, what I wanted, saying it was time for me now. She reminded me to trust my intuition, to stand on my own two feet. I immediately felt empowered to use that gut feeling to guide me. Bríd told me my grandmother, whom I'd never met, was my spirit guide, that she would help me any way she could, this made me feel very special. Bríd taught me to connect with my inner self, the part of me that instinctually knows what is right for me, to listen to my gut feeling and to stop drifting along.

Children have great imagination. With a little encouragement and repetition, they can take very well to using meditation as a form of relaxation. The following is a meditation I wrote specifically for children, but any age individual will benefit from participation.

When reading this meditation for children, I like to play some soft background music and pull down the blinds. Even though I am reciting the meditation with the intention of assisting the child, I find it also helps me relax as I let go the stresses of the day.

GUIDED MEDITATION
BEING PRESENT

Make yourself comfortable on the chair or floor.

Relax.

Notice how your body feels.

Notice your breath coming in and out of your body.

Follow the breath as it fills your entire body.

Now the air you are breathing in and out is going to go into each of your fingers one at a time.

Take a breath and imagine the air filling your right thumb (Pause) now breathe slowly out.

Now breathe in deeply letting the air fill your first finger, (Pause) then breathe slowly out.

Now the middle finger, (Pause) the 4th finger, (Pause) the little finger, (Pause) the other thumb, (Pause) the next finger, (Pause) the middle finger, (Pause) the next finger (Pause) and finally the little finger.

Breathing slowly in and slowly out.

Now take ten slow breaths with each one filling your toes. Allow the air as you breathe in and out to go into each toe one at a time.

1 2 3 4 5 6 7 8 9 10. (Pausing between each number)

Imagine your brain is a computer room with lots of computers.

Now imagine walking around that room.

Find the computer that is running.

What is the computer program saying about you?

Is what it is saying true?

If not, turn it off.

Write a true programme.

Picture yourself writing the programme using lots of coloured pencils.

I like who I am.
I am learning more about myself every day.
I am learning how to be calm.
I am learning how to be still.
Right now, I am safe.
I know I am good enough.

Now see how the rest of your body is feeling.

Is anywhere painful or uncomfortable?

How do your shoulders and back feel?

Take some deep breaths and imagine the air going into your shoulders.

Now take some deep breaths with the air going all the way down your back.

As you breathe in you feel better.

As you breathe out you relax.

You are relaxed and calm.

Know at **this moment** you are safe.

Imagine you are opening the door to your heart.

Look at the door.

How big is it?

What is it made from?

How hard is it to open?

Do you need a key?

Once you have opened the door be perfectly still for a moment.

Ask your heart *"how does it feel?"*

Is it happy or sad?

Is it hard or soft?

Know that right now you are safe.

If you are sad, know that it is ok to be sad.

It is ok to cry.

Is there a pain in your heart?

Ask your heart *"why is there a pain?"*.

When we are sad, we need to feel the sadness.

It is safe to feel sad.

It's safe to feel the pain.

It is safe to learn how to feel the pain.

Take a deep breath and fill your lungs up to the very top.

It is safe to be here now.

Think of all the things you like.

Think of the people who make you feel safe.

Think of the people you like spending time with.

Think of times that made you happy.

Think of places you felt happy.

Think of places you felt safe.

Fill your heart with pictures of all these people, places and things.

Your heart is so full you can no longer close the door.

It is safe to leave the door open.

Take another breath and let this one travel all the way down into your feet.

Again, we are going to breath into each toe. Allow the air as you breathe in and out to go into each toe one at a time.

1 2 3 4 5 6 7 8 9 10 (Pausing between each number)

It is safe to be in your body and to let your heart work.

Know that you are strong.

Know that it is also ok to be soft and gentle.

You belong on the earth.

You are supposed to be here.

I am so glad you are here.

You have a beautiful heart and you are good enough.

When you are ready, gently open your eyes – knowing you can switch on your heart when it is safe to do so.

You are in charge; you are in control of your own heart.

You are relaxed and at peace.

Now you are finding yourself back where you started.

You are returning to the waking world.

One day while doing this exercise with some children, one little girl jumped up off the floor. *"Bríd, Bríd, Bríd there is a pain. There is a pain in my heart. There is something wrong with it"*. I had been concerned for this little girl as she seemed almost permanently switched off. Now for the first time in a very long time she was connecting with her heart. I explained to her that her heart was not sick; her heart was sad.

She said she didn't like feeling this way and she didn't want to do this meditation anymore. I asked if she knew why she was sad and reassured her she didn't have to tell me her secrets. I suggested that she talk quietly to her heart about her sad things. It would help her if she could tell her heart why there was a pain. I offered to hold her hand while she was doing so. She closed her eyes tight and then started to cry. I had never seen this child cry before. My concern was that now, having opened her heart and acknowledged the pain, she may never want to repeat the process.

I explained to her that if we don't cry then all our tears will stay inside. Our heart will never feel the nice things because our heart will be full of tears. By letting out the tears there is more room for all the lovely things that happen in our lives. We can appreciate beauty and wonder; we can share love. To do so our heart must learn to reopen. That said, the child was using this

26

coping mechanism for a reason. Simply doing a meditation with her was not going to wipe out the challenging and painful encounters she experiences. When faced with these events again her safety technique of shutting down her heart is what she will need to get through those moments. We cannot advise children to put down their crutches while they still need them, not until such time as they have another support system in place.

For those of us who use this system, we need to know that we are in fact safe before switching back on. When I was a child if someone had explained to me about the coping technique I was using and asked me to switch back on my emotions, I may have done so briefly. Realising I was still emotionally overwhelmed and had to continue attending an abusive educational system, I would either have immediately shut down again, or had to find another way of coping.

If a child in your care is using this technique, before teaching them how to come back in and be present in their body; the child will need to understand their sensitivity and have other tools available to use instead.

For those who use switching off as their crutch, they may overreact to situations as they can be behind in their emotional development. Or when faced with distressing situations they may show no emotional response. The sensitive child can swap sides, going from the top half of the builder's spirit level to the lower half. Their behaviour can appear to match those on the narcissistic side, indifferent to the pain of their fellow man.

Those who do not feel emotional pain also miss out on the positive emotions in life. They can't feel excitement when something unplanned happens. They miss out on joy and spontaneity. This coping technique comes with a very high price tag. In the following story we meet John who like the girl in the meditation, had switched off all emotions as his way of coping. Prior to switching off, everyday life left him feeling overwhelmed and scared. His fears prevented him enjoying the freedom experienced by his siblings. It was some twenty-five years later before he finally let out the tears.

HONESTY IS THE BEST POLICY
JOHN

I remember when I was really young, perhaps even before the age of five, wondering why the world we lived in was so violent. Why everything seemed to be sorted out with violence. I seemed to be different from everyone around me. For example, when we were on a family day out, at a fair or some such event with loads of people around; I would be so overwhelmed. Even frightened to leave my mother's side, never letting go of her hand. As soon as my older brother and younger sister received their pocket money; they'd run off separately to go on amusement rides or whatever, but I'd stay glued to my mother.

Also, in our family I seemed to be the one affected by any disharmony between our parents. My siblings didn't seem bothered by it, whereas it bothered me a lot and I saw myself as my mother's protector. This protection wasn't only in our household, but outside the house as well, I can remember getting angry when men used to wolf-whistle and say things to my mother. Among friends, I was also the only one who would mind any younger siblings, whereas everyone else just ignored them or picked on them.

Another thing about me was that I couldn't lie. I was always honest. This used to sometimes upset people, and my mother used to say that I was just trying to cause trouble, stirring the pot. Even today I'm completely honest and people still don't like that. Whereas for me without honesty we have nothing.

Maybe around the age of five or so, I must have shut down my emotional side as a protective means to cope with this heightened sensitivity, to be able to function with all that was going on around me.

When I was 25 my emotional side came back with a massive bang. I was sitting on the couch laughing at a comedy on T.V. Then the next second, without any warning, I was on the floor having what I can only describe as a massive panic attack. For someone who had never really cried, except when I was very young, this came as a huge shock. I sat there crying my eyes out, struggling to breathe, choking and felt pain in my chest. If memory serves me well, this happened five to ten times a night for about three months. Not only was I now having to deal with the past twenty-five years' worth of undealt with emotions, but now my hyper-sensitivity was back. I was once again absorbing energy and emotions from everything and everyone around me. This was the first major shift for me, and what a rude awakening it was.

Over the years I have conversed with teenagers and young adults who have self-harmed. These have generally been female but not always. Of those I met, there seemed to be two different groups. The first group felt removed from their lives, their peers, and their experiences. They could not feel emotions. They had

30

been switched off for so long, both in their home lives and in the school or work environments. They just wanted to feel. The second group spoke of being overwhelmed by their feelings and were looking for a way of letting out the pain.

In a discussion with a teenage student who had self-harmed, we came to some surprising realisations. She described a social night out. Getting ready to go out she was very happy and excited as she and her friends put on makeup, made decisions on which clothes to wear and travelled together to the nightclub. At the club they were joined by other friends and some people she was not familiar with. As the night continued, she felt overwhelmed, feelings of insecurity and inadequacy flooded her mind. Even though she had been enjoying the evening and the company of her friends, now all she wanted to do was to leave and be on her own. She couldn't understand the conflict in her thoughts.

Completely out of character, she left the club without telling her friends. On returning to her apartment feelings of inadequacy and self-loathing overwhelmed her. This was all adding to her confused state of mind as previously she was very comfortable with her life and her companions. She described an almost out of body experience as she observed herself take a sharp knife from the kitchen and started cutting her arms. No tears fell as she watched the blood flow.

Thankfully on missing her and getting no response to their frantic phone calls, some of her friends had come in search of her. Finding her back at the apartment they offered comfort and reassurance and the feelings left. She was unable to give them, or indeed herself, any logical explanation for her actions. Her true feelings seemed to be put aside while feelings that were in no way true to her life experience took over.

I explained to her about her level of sensitivity and how in the company of others who are in strong emotional turmoil we can take on copies of their feelings. In settings where alcohol or drugs are in use, people let down their barriers and their emotional pain is even more available to those who are highly sensitive. Night clubs and discos are fun settings, full of excitement and possibilities. The music helps us relax and we generally feel safe to be present and to switch on. While switched on we are not expecting to be overcome by emotional pain. Those in our company are laughing and dancing. We forget that some are wearing a mask to hide their true feelings. With the introduction of alcohol or drugs their pain is less guarded and more available.

Alcohol can add a further level of emotional heaviness. For sensitive people who are enjoying the music and conversation, they are not expecting to suddenly feel the emotional pain of others. I explained to the teenager that this is what had happened that night when she had inflicted injuries to her arms. She had merged into the pain of someone in her company, who was struggling with feelings of inadequacy and self-loathing. Feelings of not belonging in the group's company, of not being their equal. The confused state of mind my client experienced was because these heavier emotions were in sharp conflict with her own true emotions.

EMPATHS

Traveling higher up the builder's spirit level a child's life is further impacted by their degree of sensitivity. Now they move from sensitivity to empathy. The empathic child is not just aware of the emotions of others but is actually feeling the emotional state of those in their environment. The general definition for an empath being: *"Someone who has an unusually strong ability to feel the mental and/or emotional state of another individual."*

Everything in our world is energy. Most people will assess any given situation by the evidence presented to them. They will respond based on how others are presenting. However, this is not the case for the more sensitive among us, who literally feel the energetic vibration of others. If someone is in emotional distress but has decided to hide those feelings by assuming a happy face, those in the middle of the spirit level will accept the emotion being presented. However, the sensitive person will feel the person's true vibrational distress and will often assume this new vibration as their own.

I describe this as taking a copy of someone else's emotional state and entering this copy into the sensitive child's computer. Their mind is now running two emotional programmes simultaneously. The stronger the emotion they have copied, the more likely it is to override their own programme. This can have differing results. They may assume the new programme and behave accordingly. Alternatively, they may switch, in and out, between the two programmes.

For the empath, who functions from a place of extreme sensitivity, they will be taking on more than just emotional programmes. The empath goes beyond the everyday context in which the word sensitive is usually used, i.e. someone who is compassionate to their fellow man. Some dictionaries and internet platforms can give more unexpected definitions of empaths.

"The capacity to understand or feel what another person is experiencing from within their frame of reference, that is, the capacity to place oneself in another's position".

"A person who perceives the mental or emotional state of another individual".

"A person with the paranormal ability to perceive the mental or emotional state of another individual".

Not everyone's belief system allows for the possibility of paranormal ability. Yet, those who live with this level of sensitivity are highly attuned to the feelings and emotions of those around them. This goes beyond simply having the ability to be compassionate towards the feelings of others. Understandably, science-based research is divided on whether true empaths exist. I would ask you to consider, even if this is not your own personal experience, that it is possible for some and is their everyday reality.

The empath child can assume the emotions, and/or personality, posture, behaviour, and/or physical pain of others. You may have heard parents say things like:

- *"My child completely changed when they started school".*
- *"They are a different child since they started playing with our new neighbours".*
- *"I never know what to expect from my child, happy one minute and sad the next".*

In these situations, the empathic child has taken on more than just the emotions of the other individual. Depending on who they are with - their posture, stance, walk, dialect, facial expressions and general demeanour can change to match that of their companion.

Obviously not everyone who is empathic is going to consider this ability as psychic and develop it as such. Nor should they. Everyone who is musical is not going to join the National Philharmonic Orchestra. Some may learn a few pieces of music that they happily play when no one is listening or sing their favourite song in the shower. Others will practice all day and make music their career. So it is with empathic ability, it can be developed or be kept to a minimum. Either way it is essential that it is understood, with an awareness of how to turn it on and more importantly, how to it off.

I have developed my own daily practice for disconnecting, which I call '*The Seven Steps*'. Here, I am giving a brief outline so that any caregivers whether parents, teachers, supporting staff, coaches, etc. who are themselves empathic will be able to become solid in their own energy before attempting to help children in their care. This system has been my key to unlocking my true self. It allows me to separate my programme from those of others with whom I am constantly attuned.

SEVEN STEPS
1. Tune in.
2. Check in.
3. Identify.
4. Get help.
5. Disconnect.

6. Return to own energy.
7. Express gratitude.

Step 1. Tune In.

Generally, those who are sensitive are more aware of the feelings and needs of others, rather than how they themselves are feeling. I encourage participants to take a moment to consider their own true feelings in the morning as they start their day. This becomes their reference point. *"How do I feel?"*

Step 2. Check in.

Throughout the day I regularly *'check in'* with myself and see how I am feeling **now** and observe my behaviour. I ask myself if this is in line with the events of my day. I compare it to my reference point. Are these current feelings and behaviour in accordance with the events of my day? If they are not, I know that I am in a copy of someone else's feelings/behaviour.

Step 3. Identify.

Having realised the feelings are not in line with my day; I try to identify whose energy I am picking up on. If I am feeling exhausted, for no apparent reason, I now try to identify whose company I have been in that was feeling exhausted. If I am extremely anxious, though I had felt calm earlier, then who have I met that was experiencing anxiety?

Step 4. Get help.

Personally, I believe there is a God. If you do not have a belief system, other than science and *'the here and now'*, then you can skip Step 4 and move directly on to the next step. If you have a belief system, whether Divine, angelic or universal and now, through your sensitivity, are aware someone you have had contact with is in emotional turmoil; why not ask your God to assist that person? The prayer does not need to involve a long ritual. It can be a simple but genuine sentence. *"Please God help Sarah with her anxiety". "Angels please carry David until such time as he can carry himself". "Raphael the Archangel of Healing, I ask for healing graces for Ann".*

Because of this gift, there is a realisation someone is in emotional or physical distress. If you choose to, you can pray for assistance on their behalf. It is up to the other person whether they want this assistance or not. If you believe in a higher power, then you will also believe this higher power has more understanding of the individual's *'bigger picture'* than you do.

Sometimes you will not be able to identify who you have taken the copy from and so, in this instance, the prayer can be more general. *"I ask for Divine intervention for whoever's emotions I am feeling at this time".*

When someone falls into the darkness of depression or anxiety, it is very hard to find a way out. By having their struggle brought to an empath's attention; the empath could ask on their behalf, for the light to be switched back on. They can then personally offer appropriate assistance.

Step 5. Disconnect.
It is now time to turn off the programmes which do not belong to you. There is nothing to be gained by remaining in a copy of someone else's energy for a moment longer. There are numerous ways to disconnect. Basically, you are programming your brain so that when you perform a physical movement or ritual, you are stepping out of the other person's copy and disconnecting. The simpler the technique you choose, the better. It is the intention that will make the difference. Perhaps one of the following suggestions will appeal.

- Wiping your hands on your clothes - as if you were dusting something off.
- Rubbing your hands together.
- Squeezing your hands tightly in fists, taking a breath then opening them.

- Washing your hands.
- Bringing your head slightly back to remind yourself as you face the Heavens that your higher power is now responsible.

Whatever method you choose; it is the intention that will make the difference.

Step 6. Return to one's own energy.
During any day we are likely to dust off our clothes and will be washing our hands. But, in order to return to our own energy, if we silently add some words while doing our chosen action, we are telling ourselves *"This belongs to someone else, it's now time to be me"*.

Again, you can ask for assistance from your higher power; *"I ask to return to my own energy"*. Or alternatively *"I now return to my own energy"*. It helps to say the sentence while taking a deep breath. On taking a second breath the following sentences helps the empath to feel grounded. *"I ask to return solid in my own body"* or it can be *"I return solid in my own body"*.

Whatever action and wording used; you are setting a new programme for your brain. When you follow this practice, you are no longer open to feeling the other person's emotional or physical pain. You are completely and solely in your own feelings.

41

Step 7. Express gratitude.
If your belief system allows for the appropriate intervention of a higher power, then I suggest thanking the higher power for doing so.

For children, however, this process is too long and generally beyond their comprehension. It needs to be something easy and straightforward.

The following testimonial was sent in by Teresa where she introduces us to her son. She describes him as a typical child, yet he can be deeply affected by daily events.

GRANDDAD
TERESA

Pat is probably more empathetic than sensitive. While his sister is more sensitive in terms of noise, crowds etc. Whereas Pat is a deeper thinker and feeler.

Pat is eight, he is a great kid, lots of fun, and great craic. He is a very kind boy and all his teachers say similar. He is always very helpful to kids who need a hand in school. He is also a typical eight-year-old; doesn't listen, can't find his shoes ever, loves computer games! He hates getting into any kind of trouble. If he does something he isn't allowed do, he apologises first before telling us what he has done.

Some things I have noticed over the years:

- Pat's grandfather died when he was one, so Pat has no memory of meeting him. However, he has from time to time cried about him dying and expressing how he wishes he had met him or could remember him. We brought Pat to his grandfather's grave on his request. He cherishes a picture of his grandfather and he talks about him often. We always tell him how much his grandfather loved him.

- When he heard what was happening in Ukraine, he was very upset and recommissioned an old box and started asking anyone he met to donate money to Ukraine, finally raising one hundred and thirty euro for Ukraine.

- Anything to do with animals and death he finds very upsetting. Watching one of the Jurassic movies where some of the dinosaurs got trapped on an Island and eventually died, he was so upset (even though the movie is age appropriate). Also, any movies about dogs have a similar reaction. Watching these movies allows us to open up conversations on these topics and usually a hug and a chat helps.

- He often talks about perceived slights or things he finds frustrating/annoying with some kids in his class. All very small minor things, but he finds them very annoying. They upset him to a much deeper level than one would expect. He often tells us about these things at night when he is in bed, so I ask him to tell me three really good things that have happened that day instead, which helps him calm down and go to sleep.

These children simply function at a different emotional level to most. They need child-friendly explanations; reassurance that there is nothing wrong with them, and that they are safe and accepted.

FIGHT OR FLIGHT

We are all familiar with the term '*Fight or Flight*'. This is an ingenious survival tactic the human body developed to assist the survival of our race. There is endless research available on the subject, but not specifically in relation to those who are sensitive. The term fight or flight refers to our automatic physiological reaction to any event that the body senses as being stressful or dangerous. When the mind perceives danger; it activates the sympathetic nervous system and triggers an acute stress response. This in turn prepares the body to make a best-case scenario decision on whether to fight or run away.

- The heart rate gets faster and the breathing rate increases to provide the body with the energy and oxygen needed to give a rapid response to the danger.
- A faster heartbeat increases oxygen flow to the major muscles.
- Pain perception drops.
- Extra hormones including cortisol are produced.

- The person's hearing sharpens.
- Pupils will dilate to enable additional light to enter and improve vision.

This wonderful technique our ancestor the '*cave man*' developed obviously works, as humans have continued to increase in number. Whatever threat he was faced with, be it a dangerous animal or competing against other tribes, his automatic physiological reaction enabled him to assess the imminent danger. In this heightened state of awareness, he could decide whether to run or stay and fight. If he decided to run, even if injured, his pain perception had lessened allowing him to escape. When safe, he would start to feel the true level of pain. When on alert his hearing levels sharpened, listening mainly to louder and quieter sounds. While in danger the brain does not consider everyday sounds to be a priority. Whereas the roar of a bear or the enemy sneaking up behind him was a real threat.

Unfortunately, there is a flaw in our fight or flight strategy. It reacts the same to perceived danger as it does to actual danger. If our ancestor was tucked up safely at night in his cave and started to think about the '*what ifs*' his body would perceive this as a threat. While lying comfortably, ready to drift off to sleep, his mind goes to all the possible dangers that could happen the following day:

- *"What if I meet a bear when I don't have my stick with its sharp edge with me?"*
- *"What if another cave man steals my mate?"*
- *"What if there is a storm and all the berries blow off the trees?"*
- *"What if I can't get the fire to light and I won't be able to cook dinner?"*

When the mind starts to do *'what ifs'* or listing all that we have done wrong that day, we can put ourselves into a state of anxiety. By concentrating on the *'what ifs'* *'should haves'* and *'shouldn't haves'* the body goes into the same responses as when facing imminent danger. While lying safely tucked in and thinking of all the *'what ifs'* the caveman's mind starts to assess and determine if there is danger. *"Well, I can't see a bear or enemy, but I'm really stressed so there must be a danger here somewhere".*

The sensitive child's life is completely unpredictable. Happy one moment then sad for no apparent reason. They are unable to control their emotions from one moment to the next. The tools many will have developed to help them cope with their challenges, often lead to further complications. Similar to some long-term medication where the side effects

47

can outweigh the positive benefits. For them the *'what ifs'* can take over:

- *"What if when I am happy, I suddenly feel sad and start crying?"*
- *"What if I start crying and people laugh at me?"*
- *"What is going to happen tomorrow that I need to be ready for?"*
- *"What if the teacher uses the projector and the lights hurt my eyes?"*
- *"What if I can't cope and bite or hit someone?"*
- *"What if things are out of order?"*
- *"What do I need to do to make sure the grownups aren't cross with me?"*
- *"What is going to happen next?"*
- *"What are all the things I did wrong today that I need to get right tomorrow?"*
- *"How can I be more like the other children?"*

Constantly living in a state of fight or flight, is one of the potential consequences of being sensitive. This perceived danger mode plays havoc with the child's body. Generally, the extra cortisol will be used up during the daily activities, running, jumping, and climbing. Cortisol is essential to help control blood pressure, increase the body's metabolism of glucose, and reduces inflammation. But when the child is stressed and doesn't have playtime activities - then the hormone is not getting used. If we have too much cortisol in our system - we overreact to common stressors resulting in emotional outbursts. For children who are not active during the day, the body must find a way of using the cortisol or find somewhere to store it. The liver tends to be its first option; following on from there it will look to store the excess hormone in other soft tissue organs. This leads on to other medical problems and further strain on the body.

Many children will run their anxiety programme before going to sleep. They may go back through their interactions of the day. Trying to understand their responses to various events. Some will endeavour to come up with ways to get it right tomorrow. Often this is a highly self-critical assessment. In this programme the child eventually drifts off to sleep. As they do so they have just started the fight or flight process. One part of this involves the production of cortisol. During sleep this hormone is not going to be used and generally results in the child waking in the middle of the night and struggling to get back to sleep.

Their system is ready for action, to run from danger. But they are not running. Their exhausted parent/guardian, who may frequently have to get up at night to a child who is wide awake, will struggle to get them back to sleep. Telling someone who is pumping cortisol "*GO BACK TO SLEEP*" really is not going to work. As the child attempts to get back to sleep they may return to their usual practice of running their critical anxiety programme in their mind. "*I've woke up mammy, she is cross with me*". This starts the whole process again. When it is finally time to get up and face the world, their body has not rested sufficiently. This now adds to their daily challenges. If their parent/guardian is tired, grumpy, and frustrated from lack of sleep the sensitive child will soak up these emotions and add them on top of their own.

In a state of perceived danger, the digestive system is affected. The central nervous system shuts down digestion by slowing contractions of digestive muscles and decreasing secretions for digestion. If in long term fight or flight, the digestive system will get used to being sluggish and functioning with slow metabolism. The normal production of vitamins, minerals and nutrients produced from food is compromised. In effect, the child is putting fuel into their human vehicle, but it is not reaching their engine. It is not uncommon to lose voluntary control of the bladder or bowel in a truly stressful or dangerous situation. Spending large amounts of time in this heightened state is difficult for anyone. The sensitive child, who is already frequently overwhelmed, must now contend with taking on a seemingly hostile world with their tank in the red. Adding to their worries they may now suffer: stomach cramps, constipation, or diarrhoea. In prolonged states of anxiety, without sufficient nutrient absorption, concentration is affected. Extreme stressful situations can result in memory loss. Normal growth can be stunted.

The child may seem pale or have flushed skin. The blood flow is being redirected so they might experience feeling cool, or their hands and feet may be cold and clammy. Their face might also appear flushed as blood and hormones circulate throughout the body.

In their daily lives the sensitive child will feel agitated around children who are loud, aggressive or in various states of emotional turmoil. They will look for ways to try to protect themselves from being overwhelmed. Their coping technique in these challenging moments may be to physically attack, bite or lash out at whoever they feel is putting them in danger. Any understanding of the true level of pain their body is experiencing is compromised as their pain perception drops. In heightened anxiety they may only feel their own injuries once the body deems it is safe to do so. Sometimes sensitive children hit out at other children who overwhelm them. They are being bombarded by these strong emotions or the noise of raised voices are literally hurting them. Their solution to stopping their discomfort may be to make the offender stop, by whatever means necessary.

Normally if we were to hit someone with our hand it will hurt us as well as them. If the other child hits back that will also hurt. In fight or flight this is not the case. If the 'aggressor' is not feeling pain, they may continue their attack. To the supervising adult it is obvious who the aggressor is, and they must be reprimanded accordingly. The sensitive child will now also absorb the annoyance of the adult and adds this in on top of all they are already trying to deal with. For them their day is now all about survival. They may try to run away, or kick out at the adult, the wall or anything in the vicinity. They are overwhelmed and somehow need to detach from all the emotions. They also need to use up the cortisol. It is not until their system has calmed, that they will start to be aware of their own physical pain from their encounter. As the aggressor they are unlikely to be awarded the comfort and reassurance normally available to a hurt child.

Like our ancestor, the cave man, who was on alert for dangerous animals and enemies; when we find ourselves in fight or flight our hearing sharpens. The child in anxiety will be more aware of loud noise and raised voices. They will also hear very low sounds that others may not hear. When trying to sleep they may hear the hum of the fridge in the kitchen, or a dripping tap - while others are oblivious to these sounds. Even in sleep, they may wake to the sound of a creaking floorboard as the boards adjust to the night-time drop in temperature. During the day they will hear the smallest of sounds and will become distracted.

While in this state, concentration is compromised. Added to this they are now prioritising loud and low sounds over normal conversation. If the parent/guardian, or teacher is speaking in their normal tone, this child will not be actively listening. They will be listening for loud and/or quiet sounds. If this continues people may get frustrated. *"You are not listening to me". "Have you heard anything I have been saying?" "Are you daydreaming again?"*

Recently a mother brought her fourteen-year-old son to meet me. This teenager is highly sensitive to his environment and often becomes overwhelmed. Participating in large groups is very difficult for him. He has been struggling in school, especially in maths class and was considering moving back to a lower-level class in several of his subjects. He was convinced that he was not as intelligent as his peers.

He was relieved when I explained to him what was going on. In primary school he had managed to keep up academically with his class, as his mother had spent time teaching him the basics in his subjects. He was completely relaxed at home and had heard his mum's explanations.

His primary education had been in a small country school and he was able to cope. On moving to secondary, he went from a class of ten children to a class of thirty children. This meant he was constantly bombarded by emotions. In class he was frequently in fight or flight mode. When the maths teacher would start to write on the board, he was not hearing her explanations. He was looking at what she had written but without the verbal explanations he was at a serious disadvantage.

Understanding his sensitivity and the effect his anxiety was having on him, helped him realise his intellect was not the problem. I reassured him that he was in fact very clever to have managed to comprehend as much as he had done, without the verbal explanations the other children were hearing. Most of the subjects e.g., History, Geography, English, involved reading and learning from the books and then retaining this information. Maths required detailed explanation from the teacher, much of which he had not heard.

After he left, I had a flash back to my own experiences in school. Following this conversation, I now had a new understanding of what had happened when I was in fifth class, aged ten.

LONG DIVISION

I had always struggled with my reading and spellings and was used to getting punished for these mistakes. However, I had always done well in maths. Irrespective of what else was happening with alternating emotions, mistreatment, and fear; two plus two was always four. When doing maths my concentration was completely focused. This was the one subject in which I always achieved high scores.

One day we turned to a new chapter in our maths books, Long Division. The nun went to the board and drew a long line with a semicircle attached at the lower left-hand side. She wrote a double number outside and a triple number inside. Then she started writing numbers above the line and numbers below the triple number. Every so often she would include a single number in tiny writing. Homework was set for a page of these mysterious and perplexing long division calculations.

Not surprisingly, the following day I had every answer wrong. The nun was furious with me. She called me to the front of the room and told me to do the first sum on the board. I made some efforts but had no understanding of the task. She started shouting names at me. Then catching me by my shoulders, banged my head back against the board. I was then instructed to redo the task correctly. I was some forty years younger than her but knew if I didn't understand it before she whacked my head - chances were, I still didn't. I felt fear, injustice, anger and frustration. In hindsight, much of the frustration and anger was probably hers.

The light bulb moment I had was that I would have been in extreme anxiety. In fight or flight my hearing would have been compromised for much of my school time. Up to this I had solved the maths myself. Two plus two I could count on my fingers or ten take away seven I could solve. This was the first time when maths needed detailed explanation from the nun. While doing this, she had her back to the class. In fight or flight, I had simply not heard her words. Normal tones were generally not a danger. When she was shouting or quietly pulling back her chair – these were dangerous moments. These had become the priority sounds. I had simply not heard the explanation. I now understand why that maths chapter proved so difficult and so dangerous.

Sensitive people start off in life as soft, gentle, and caring. They prioritise the needs of others over their own needs and have a strong desire to people please. Their mind is over stimulated in their effort to ensure everyone's safety and happiness. This hypervigilance and over stimulation can leads to anxiety. This anxiety pushes them into a state of fight or flight.

COMING OFF THE CLIFF

The anxious child will be on edge, more aware of their surroundings and more observant of small details. They will subconsciously be looking and listening for things that could be dangerous. Not only are they on alert for dangers to themselves, but they are also hyper-vigilant of dangers to others. Their senses are heightened, and they are keenly aware of what is going on around them. They will prioritise danger over the everyday activities that others concentrate on. Their nervous system will be strained, their bodies tense. They will be rigid. In this space there is little scope for tolerance. They may appear to overreact to inconsequential events. Instead of their normal gentle, caring self they now have little patience or tolerance for others. In their anxiety they can be perceived as difficult, distracted, violent, selfish, and uncaring. If they continue to live in a state of anxiety, they can become the aggressor.

Once a child understands their sensitivity and has the tools and a vocabulary for daily use, they will no longer feel so overwhelmed. This will then reduce their anxiety programme. Those who are prone to anxiety tend to run their programme at night. Therefore, this is a particularly good time to address the pattern. If you have ever participated in rock climbing or seen people mountaineering, you will be aware that total concentration is needed. Every movement needs to be carefully considered. The body is tense - with tension in the neck, arms, and legs. While in this state, one is not going to stop to meditate or listen to relaxing music on their earphones. Before relaxation is possible the climber first needs to get off the cliff to safety. Then they can readjust their breathing and participate in relaxation techniques. If someone is clinging to the cliff by their fingertips there is no point shouting at them to relax. The same applies to those in heightened anxiety. They need to come off the cliff before they can relax.

When a child is in anxiety, they need encouragement from someone they trust before releasing their death grip on the ledge. One way to do this is with the introduction of positive reinforced sentences. If you are aware of their personal beliefs or struggles; relate them to the following sentences. It will be beneficial if this can happen periodically but especially at night.

- *"You really tried today".*
- *"I know it's hard and I'm proud of you".*
- *"It was a tough day and you did your best".*

- *"You've got through up to this point".*
- *"Let's wipe the slate clean and start again".*
- *"Tomorrow is a new day".*
- *"You did really well at the xxxx task".*
- *"You are learning so much".*
- *"You have a huge heart".*
- *"You know you are loved".*
- *"There are so many wonderful experiences waiting for you".*
- *"The best days of your life are still to come".*

Whatever sentences are being used they need to be real and believable. You are trying to convince the child to turn off their anxiety programme and come off the cliff. If you can identify something the child has done well in that day or even where there has been a slight improvement - this will help the child to feel better about their endeavours. It needs to be real. If the child has been suspended or expelled from school for a physical outburst that day, there is no point saying, *"today was a lovely day"*. They need reassurance but it needs to be credible. Remember for this child life is a constant struggle.

I had the privilege of observing an SNA (Special Needs Assistant) working with a young child of perhaps eight years of age. The little girl was in constant anxiety and was behind for her age in both academic and social skills. The assistant asked the girl to write the numbers one to ten. After some encouragement the child reluctantly did as instructed. I looked at what she had written and wondered what numbers the squiggles were meant to represent. Looking at the child's endeavours the SNA praised her while focusing in on the number six. She explained how some children struggle with the number six and make a straight line instead of a curve, ending up with the letter b, whereas this child had curved the number correctly. The little girl was so pleased. She was not used to praise and believed herself incapable of ever learning how to read or do maths. With this SNA's encouragement, life for this child began to improve. With anxious children we need to find their 'sixes'. By finding positives, that are real and specific, rather than *you are a great girl*' they will begin to believe themselves capable and begin to move off the cliff.

Once the child is calm **then** relaxation techniques can be put in place.

- Introducing a new night-time routine with soft music or nursery rhymes.
- Breathing exercises.
- Sitting quietly with them in their room while they fall asleep.

Often the parent/guardian is so sleep deprived due to the child waking frequently, that they themselves just want to go to bed. If the child can break the pattern of the way their mind over-analyses, before falling asleep, the whole household will benefit.

If your interaction with sensitive children is in a classroom setting, there are endless mindfulness options available. Again, it's important to remember that while the child remains on the cliff these options won't work. Before they can participate in relaxation techniques the child needs to know they are safe, and that the danger at this time is perceived rather than real.

It is important to realise that when any distressed child is in the proximity of a sensitive child - **both** children will need extra attention. For example, if a little girl has fallen and is crying because she has hurt her knee, she will need the appropriate assistance and reassurance. The sensitive child, who has witnessed the little girl's distress, will also be upset. As they have taken on a copy of the little girl's emotions and will need assistance to disconnect and to return to a calm state of being. Some will even have taken on a copy of the shock and physical pain the girl experienced.

One technique that may benefit all children is the '*Red Dot*' breathing exercise. Red dots are placed in key locations throughout the building. Children are taught to breathe deeply in through their nose and out through their mouth on seeing the dots. These can be placed on the entrance door to the building, on the bathroom sink or mirror, on the top corner of the white board in the classroom or wherever seems appropriate. It becomes a normal routine for all the children (and perhaps the adults). When any child is in physical or emotional difficulty, the adult in charge simply points to the dot. All the children in the room then concentrate on their breathing and avoid getting pulled into the drama of the event.

This can be repeated between subjects. When a child feels challenged by a particular subject e.g., maths, a red dot can be added to the cover of the child's maths books. Once it becomes a part of their daily routine, it helps them to stay grounded and avoid fight or flight. Obviously, this technique on its own will not prevent anxiety but it adds a practical tool. Not just for the sensitive child but for all the children in the classroom. Everyone will experience anxiety from time to time and learning simple mindfulness techniques from an early age means these become an everyday part of life. Less stress means better concentration and participation.

This technique can also be used in a home setting. The dot can be on the bedside locker, or chest of drawers. On the inside of the car door where the child sits, or in the bathroom. For older children perhaps it can be added to the cover of their mobile phone or tablet.

If a child has gone into fight or flight, they will need to work off the extra hormones. Otherwise, they will remain hyperactive/wired. During class time this may be difficult to organise. Perhaps they could be asked to run around the school and check how many windows are open or how many empty car spaces there are in the yard or if the flag is flying correctly. By making it look as if they are being of assistance; they will not feel singled out. Nor will others see it like that. Following any emotional outburst, young children may all benefit from some physical activity.

Likewise, at home, once the school day is over the child may need to *'burn off steam'* (cortisol) before they can concentrate on homework or any household task. It doesn't need to be an entire football match; a few minutes doing jumping jacks, skipping, even jogging on the spot will help them to use up the extra hormones being produced from their stress.

GUIDED MEDITATION
COMING OFF THE CLIFF

Make yourself comfortable – relaxing into your chair (or on the floor)

Become aware of your breathing.

Be aware of what you are thinking.

It is safe to turn off the negative thoughts.

Know you are good enough.

You are capable and have always been capable.

You are a sensitive, caring, gentle person with a beautiful heart and you are good enough.

Yesterday is done and tomorrow will take care of itself, as it always does.

Step out of the past – step out of the future.

It is safe to relax and to allow your eyelids to float closed.

It is time to allow your shoulders to relax and let the tension held there loosen.

Let your jaw un-clinch, the muscles in your arms and legs release.

It is safe to come off the cliff.

Allowing your tummy to break down its food, your gut to function.

It is time to allow your body to receive its nutrients, vitamins, and minerals.

It is safe to be well.

Bring your awareness back to the breath, back to your breathing.

Observe your breath moving in and out of your body, your chest rise and fall.

Each breath relaxing, calming, and soothing your body.

Breathe out all the tension and stress.

Where in your body do you notice the breath after it enters through your nose?

Your throat, your heart, your chest, your tummy?

Continue to pay attention to your breath.

Knowing your negative computer programmes have now been switched off.

It is safe to breathe.

Again, notice the breath moving through your body.

Know **right now** you are safe.

You are calm.

Observing the space where your breath enters and leaves.

When you are ready gently open your eyes – knowing you can switch off the programme.

You are in charge.

You are in control of your own mind.

SENSORY OVERLOAD

For children with severe learning difficulties, expression can be challenging. The more limiting their condition the more limited their options for expression. To an observer their reactions may seem extreme. But the more distressed the child, the greater the need for expression. Their response can range from rapid eye movement to full physical assault. For children who are unable to express in words what they are experiencing - a physical outburst may be the only way they can communicate their distress. For those of us fortunate not to have these restrictions it is incomprehensible to imagine living in a world without communication. Even worse if we lacked the ability to communicate and those around us had no experience or understanding of this challenge.

The home and family unit may be the entire world to some children. The smallest of changes, within daily routine, can result in feelings of uncertainty. What may seem insignificant or inconsequential to others can unsettle these children. If they are highly sensitive, they will be aware of the emotions of those they spend their time with. The more sensitive the child, the more they will be impacted by any and every change in their environment. The higher their level of sensitivity, the greater they will be impacted. Some may respond physically, some verbally or for those without these abilities, they may express through their gut.

When faced with fear or anxiety they may become constipated or have diarrhoea. In extremely difficult situations they may express through vomiting. With their gut in a frequent state of stress, they struggle to break down their foods. This results in a lack of essential nutrients which their body needs to function. Their weakened and vulnerable bodies are now further challenged. If a sensitive child is then reprimanded for their outburst, in addition to their own emotional distress, they can take on a copy of the feelings of frustration, exhaustion and stress of their carer.

Life for all parents presents many challenges. Identifying the needs of the child and how to meet those needs; finding balance between the desires of the child, and what is in their best interest. Their children are often their main thought and concern. These challenges are all the greater when a child has special needs. Many parents will spend their days caring for and assisting these children. They become the voice and advocate for their offspring. For many, this child becomes the central focus and the child's needs are often their full-time concern. It is not possible for any caregiver to be present twenty-four seven for their child. Everyday life will interrupt. There may be a necessity to work or attend to other family matters. Decisions may need to be made around education or additional care providers. When a caregiver's routine changes, their first concern will be how this will impact their child. Understandably the adult will be anxious as to how the child will react to changes in their normal routine.

- *"How will they get on with the person who is stepping in to provide care?"*
- *"How will they behave at their new school?"*
- *"Will they become overwhelmed and react physically?"*
- *"Will the child minder be able to understand their needs?"*
- *"Will the school reduce the level of time allotted to the child if they have physical outbursts?"*
- *"Will the child minder come back?"*
- *"Will the child be upset afterwards and take ages to settle?"*
- *"Will the child be physical towards the parent on their return?"*
- *"Is it easier just to decline the wedding invitation?"*

Being so used to speaking on their child's behalf and anticipating their every need, the parent is now handing their precious, vulnerable child to someone else. The child will pick up on this anxiety and will respond with whatever means their body allows. It will not be easy, but it is vital that caregivers move beyond guilt and realise it is essential to practice and model self-care. By allowing others to help, the exhausted parent can step out and be rejuvenated, even if for a very limited time. In guilt this is not possible. Having stepped out, if done without guilt they will have briefly shifted their focus to their own needs. The sensitive child will be aware the parent's energy is re-energised and calmer. In this space new thoughts can take over.

- *"It was lovely to step out and take time for myself".*
- *"I must do this more often".*
- *"I need to find a way to do this more often".*

All children have different levels of emotional sensitivity as the example of the builder's spirit level demonstrates. Now add to this the various senses: smell, hearing, taste, touch, and sight. Each of these senses can be impacted to varying degrees. This will vary depending on the person and by how solid they are in their own energy, at any given time.

A child may have sensitive hearing, this is in addition to the fact they may be in fight or flight. Certain sounds may cause irritation or even hurt them. To others this may simply present as everyday background noise. But for a child with sensitive hearing this will be a challenge. The sound of writing with chalk or marker on a board, traffic passing by outside, a vehicle with reversing beepers, a toilet flushing, even someone clicking a biro can cause irritation or pain in extreme hearing sensitivity. The more the child is affected by these sounds, the more reactive their response. Ear plugs or simply wearing a hairband over their ears or a hat, a hoodie, or headphones, may lessen the distress. While for others anything touching their ears can cause irritation.

Similarly, there are challenges for those who are light sensitive. They can be uncomfortable sitting by a window or anywhere there is light reflection. Glare from the sun in the car windscreen or from oncoming traffic can stress the child's system. They may feel like they are in a hostile environment before they even start a challenging school day.

In the classroom, lights from a projector or photocopier can add further distress. Once aware of this challenge, steps can be put in place. Glasses that are anti-glare and/or have a colour tint added, may reduce the stress on eyes. Perhaps relocate the child's desk, placing them with their back to the window or at an angle to the projector. Instead of the child being instructed to observe the whiteboard or projector, hand notes can be provided.

For others, foods can be a challenge. Some don't like how certain foods **feel** in their mouth. Tomatoes, onions, mushrooms, cabbage, and peppers are common examples of such foods. Many adults will never have considered that for some, the texture of certain foods makes them feel sick. Vegetables are good for us, part of our '*five a day*'. But mealtime will become a very anxious time, when a child is instructed to eat something, they physically can't bring themselves to put in their mouth. This can in turn lead on to further problems.

PLAY TIME

When I was in primary school the two best times of the day were when the bell went for lunch time and when the bell went for going home. However, the temporary reprieve of lunch time presented new challenges. The biggest challenge was the retired nun who covered yard duties. At the time she seemed the oldest person I had ever met. But she packed a mean punch.

To meet the needs of the poor, the nuns had decided to provide *'food'* for the students. The ancient nun would bring a tray of slices of white, yeast bread with a thin coating of jam, into the school yard. The bread must have been prepared the previous evening as it was completely dried out. The crust was charcoal black. Generally, to my recollection, every child had their own lunch. However, if she gave you bread, you had to eat it. Otherwise, she would physically reprimand you.

There was no point explaining that you had eaten your lunch and were not hungry. *"No thank you"* was not an option. In fact, any reply other than *"Thank you"* resulted in a reprimand and you would still have to take the bread. It tasted stale and dry. There was nowhere to dispose of it as: our uniforms had no pockets, there were no bins, the walls were too high to throw it over and if you tried to flush it down the toilet it floated!

I could just about force down the bread, but however I tried, I simply could not swallow the crust. No matter what I did with it, how long I chewed it, broke it up and wrapped the stale white bread around it, I just couldn't swallow the crust. The texture and taste resulted in a desire to vomit. To this day hard black crust brings back school memories.

For children who do not like how certain food feels, no matter how hard they try to please the adult, it may not be possible to swallow without becoming nauseous.

Clothing textures can be a trigger for others. A mum described to me how difficult it is to shop for her little boy. At this stage she waits for him to accompany her. He needs to know how the item *'feels.'* He will literally place the item of clothing against his face. Some he will discard immediately, though moments earlier he may have been all excited about the colour or design. He needs to feel the item against his skin, this also applies to underwear, socks, bedlinen, towels, and swim wear. His mum has learnt there is no point surprising him with new clothes. He needs to be included in the process or he may not be able to wear them.

She also described the *'nightmare'* of shoe shopping for this child. This can take an entire day. The shoes need to be in a pattern with his existing shoes before he will even try them on. Unfortunately, he is unable to explain the pattern. They walk from shop to shop as he studies the shoes. It may be a shoe with similar colours, or the same number of eyelets for laces, perhaps on that day the pattern is the make of shoe. Finally, having found something that lines up in pattern - he then must try it on to see how it feels. If he does not like the feel of his choice, the search continues.

Some people reading this may think this is just encouraging the child to be difficult. However, if forced into wearing something where the material or pattern is the cause of irritation the child will be distressed prior to even leaving their home. Their day will be more challenging than necessary. Similarly, if we were given clothes made from straw to wear, the discomfort it would cause throughout the day would prove unbearable. There can still be parameters set when shopping. *"This is the budget. This is what you are allowed, and this is what you are not allowed"*.

The following testimonial was sent in by Florence. Her daughter has faced many challenges and has found her own ways of dealing with these difficulties - in the absence of a society which provides the tools and explanations needed.

SOCKS
FLORENCE

I have two daughters. Both are now wonderful young adults, living largely independent lives. From the moment each was born I was wrapped into their needs, their personalities, their ways in the world. They are the ones who taught me almost all I know about love.

One of them is very sensitive in her own particular ways. While I would say everyone in sensitive, I now recognise that in some people that sensitivity goes further, and manifests in particular ways. I'm not sure I saw it in my daughter when she was very young. I was immersed in doing the parenting thing as best I could and, while she had her own personal demands and behaviours, I did not automatically think she was unusual in her sensitivities. I did what every parent tries to do – meet her needs.

There were some challenging times when she was young. For example, she only ate a limited range of not particularly healthy foods. With hindsight, I can see that the *fussy eater* was displaying an aspect of her sensitivities. We now know she has a number of food intolerances, and she manages her own healthy diet within these parameters. She also has sensory issues with certain food textures, which make them almost impossible to eat without gagging. How many people judge a young fussy eater and comment how his/ her parents are bringing the problem on themselves by not being strict enough? Think again.

Clothes could also be an issue when she was young, and it could take a while to get her dressed. Again, with hindsight, I can see her acute sensory sensitivity meant that it took some time to get clothes feeling '*right*' (for example, the seams on the inside of the toes on socks). She often preferred no clothes – a wise child! Nowadays she has a fantastic dress sense, and I have never thought to ask her about whether she chooses clothes based on how they '*feel*' – it might be interesting to hear what she has to say.

Now she is older and can articulate her experiences and needs very well. I have heard her say, that some people make her feel that she is being difficult and awkward when she doesn't conform to their idea of how she is '*meant*' to be in the world. Often it is well-intentioned adults with rigid ideas (that category would include me at times!!), and it comes across as disempowering. It can be particularly tricky for her to negotiate when that adult has some authority over her. She has taught me that I need to listen actively to her (rather than being on autopilot), and to respect her autonomy and way of being in the world. This dynamic of one person shutting down another and not listening to or respecting them is recognisable to all of us. But where there are extreme sensitivities involved it can be particularly acute. I often feel like shouting loudly to let all young people know: "*You are right! Don't let those adults dismiss your experiences and blithely rationalise your feelings away as if they are wrong!*"

At the same time, while I make a case for listening to people with sensitivities and respecting their needs, I also know that a sensitive person can be on overload for much of their lives, and not have the capacity to offer others much room for their particular needs. Ha! It goes in circles! My own mother had extreme sensitivities and was often not available to me as a young child. Bríd named these family sensitivities to me, and it helped me have compassion for my mother's version of doing her best for her children.

By naming my daughter as extremely sensitive, Bríd helped enormously. My daughter said to me later that day, "*I didn't know it was a thing*". It started us down a new road of making sense of how she was in the world, and what to do about it. My sensitive daughter struggled with her mental health, particularly in her mid-teens. It was very hard to watch as a parent. My protective instinct leapt to the surface, yet it was her path to walk with her own inner resources to wellness. My own anxiety patterns caused me at times to jump in to meet my idea of her needs uninvited or brought an extra level of '*hyper-ness*' to the atmosphere. Bríd, and others, helped me to see my own patterns, which I then started to address.

I am now much more aware of how a single fear can instantly cloud my mind. I also know the relief and strength that arises when I have put any fears in their appropriate place and am better able to respond to challenging situations with calmness and clarity. I recently took another step, based on recognising my own particular sensitivity as an empath (thank you Bríd). For me as an empath, it feels natural to merge with my children at some level as a way of *'being with them'*. At times this gives me valuable insight. However, I now recognise that this can get in the way of letting my children develop fully into their own selves, in their own right. Also, if I in effect, *'join them'*, then I lose the chance of being genuinely clear and available to them, and it can lead to issues being magnified rather than calmly addressed. I am now better able to maintain my energetic independence from them as needed. Essentially, I am more myself for more of the time, which allows them to be more themselves more of the time. This learning has had a wonderful effect on all my relationships.

I greatly admire my sensitive daughter for how she gets up and gets on with her day; despite the extra demands that her sensitivity puts her under. I saw this first when she was younger, when her almost constant runny nose and allergies would tire her out physically, yet she still managed to keep up with others around her. Now she's older, I can also see her responding to the heightened mental and emotional demands with her best foot forward. Fair play to her. She's amazing.

The more grounded the child is in their own energy, the less they will be impacted by their environment. Their anxiety will be further lessened if they, are fortunate to have caregivers who are understanding of their unique individual challenges. This doesn't mean caregivers must have all the answers. It will be helpful if the adults can listen to the child's language e.g. *'I don't like how this tomato feels' 'I can't sleep with the new pillowcase' 'this isn't in pattern'* and discuss the possible options/alternatives. For all of us, just knowing someone cares can make such a positive difference to our day.

Many will adopt the use of order as a tool to cope with life's challenges. They may be overwhelmed by emotion, noise, touch, taste, or light, but they can control and understand order. This may be something as simple as the order their clothes go in the wardrobe or their toys position on a shelf. It may extend to the order they wear their clothes, what colour socks on which day, the position their shoes are placed in, the cup or plate they use for their dinner, the order their books go in their school bag. They may be unable to control their senses and their emotions, which are constantly overwhelming them. But they can decide which book goes where on the bookshelf. This helps us understand the child who needs to live in patterns.

Unfortunately, the need for order tends to increase as their challenges grow. This tool, which they originally adopted to help them feel calm, knowing that when life is out of control their possessions will always be in order, can start to work against them. As life presents further challenges, being in the presence of people whose emotions and behaviour cannot be put in order, they try to control more aspects of their own life by putting further controls in place.

When at school, one little boy was unable to line up with the other children as they awaited the school bell. He believed the line was not in the correct order. He thought the child who was at the front of the line yesterday, should be at the back of the line today. The child who was second in the line yesterday should be in the front of the line today and so on. But the school policy was that children join the queue as they arrived at school. The little boy simply could not do this, as he felt physically ill by the perceived lack of order.

There are many such challenges for children who use order as a coping mechanism. For example, when children are asked to run an errand to another room, the teacher may choose a child who had finished a task. Whereas the order-based child has a very specific rule for who should be sent. There is a myriad of daily minefields: playing sports, lining up to run a race or queue for the school bus, being split into groups for activities etc. Most children simply go with the order presented. The order-based child will be traumatised by the disregard for '*proper*' rules.

For those who have adapted their lives using this coping tool, it will take time and understanding before they can let this go. If someone is dependent on a crutch to walk, taking it away and telling them to "*just walk*" will not work - without first putting other supports in place. This person may need therapy as they adjust to life without their crutch.

Criticising or punishing a child, for their need for order, will not help them adjust to the view of the majority. They introduced this tool for a reason. It was their safety net, for when they fell off the tightrope. The child will need to come off the tightrope before their safety net is removed, or a new safety net will be needed in its place.

Ultimately no caregiver can always be in a positive mental frame of mind. It is sufficient to know they have done the best they could at any given time. We will all look back at occasions through critical eyes but at the time we did the best we could with what was available. These children are guilty of no crime. Nor are their parents. In the absence of understanding, assistance and guidelines, caregivers are navigating as best they can in often extremely difficult circumstances.

UNZIP THE CLOUD
ANONYMOUS

A woman?   Yes.
A daughter? Yes.
A sister?   Yes.
An aunt?   Yes.
A wife?   Yes
A mother?   Yes

Yes! I am all of these. So, I'm an expert on all things female? Wrong! On one level, I can revel in the fact that I am a keen multi-tasker. However, it comes at a great cost to my mental and physical wellbeing. All too often I walk around under a cloud of '*should haves*' and '*should nots*'. Second-guessing what the right thing to do is and in my search for the '*right*' answer, speak to my nearest and dearest and actively listen to their opinions. Soaking it all in and replaying their instructions in my subconscious.

But doing exactly that, caused mayhem internally for me. Not quite at the level of a breakdown – I like to refer to it as an *'unzipping of my cloud'*. Thanks to a dear friend who took the time to actually hear my silent struggle, I took up her suggestion to meet Bríd. Before I had time to deliberate, I was on my way to North Clare.

I was welcomed by beautiful scenery and a wholesome, spiritual person. My time with Bríd allowed me to unzip my cloud. Pourings of tears, trapped inside of me for nearly six years, trickled. What brought me to her, she asked. I didn't really know the answer. Yes, my friend suggested it, but I knew deeply that I needed some spiritual unearthing.

What had I kept safely blocked up inside me? Lots! Fear of doing the wrong thing; letting down my family or worse doing the wrong thing for my son, who has additional needs. The ghostly words etched silently in my mind's eye over the last few years since his diagnosis: *"Don't label him"*, *"No need to tell anyone"*, *"He might grow out of it"*, translated to me as: Keep it hidden, deal with it yourself and if you're good enough, nobody will ever know about it.

Bríd guided me to the sacred place, where I took an introspective look at myself and my thoughts.

She verbalised what I really needed to hear: "*Your son has done nothing wrong; you and your husband have nothing to hide, you have a wonderful son. He is autistic and he is lucky to have you as his mum. Release it. There's nothing to hide. You can do this*".

Yes! I have nothing to hide. He is beautiful. Both my sons are equally wonderful and wondrous. Freedom at last. Free from the shackles of other people's opinions. Free from self-imposed entrapment.

My journey to Bríd set me on a road I may never have known existed or, worse, may never have dared travel. Self-belief and ridding myself of carrying others' insecurities have helped me unzip my cloud. It is a journey, however, and I've lots more to travel. To Bríd I owe a huge "*Thank You*".

ANGER ISSUES

Everyone has '*triggers*', memories or behaviours that impact them more than others. Generally, people are impacted most by the emotions they encountered in childhood. If a family member suffered from depression; this is the emotion that will have the most impact when encountered outside of the home. When someone is hypersensitive these triggers impact to a greater level. Their energy levels will drop as will their enthusiasm. They will behave as if they are suffering depression.

When a sensitive person is unfortunate enough to have a family member who is abusive, aggressive, controlling, or with addiction, then this is the energy they will be quickest to absorb and respond to. When the child is presented with someone who is angry, they absorb this strong emotion and allow it to override their own programme. They may now behave in an angry manner. Their emotions become a mirror image of the person they have just encountered; they may react to the anger they are absorbing with similar behaviour.

In the following story we meet Dara. To cope with the emotional pain of his surroundings, he put on a hard exterior. As others encountered this tough kid, they accepted this projection as Dara's true self. But his truth was hidden underneath. It took a very determined teacher to provide a safe space and encourage the genuine child to emerge.

DARA
MÁIRE

Dara came to our school aged seven. He was a product of a broken marriage and experienced trauma as a result of emotional, physical, domestic and alcohol abuse. He was the second of three children in the family. When Dara was abandoned by his mother, his father decided to move from the family home in Dublin with the children. Things should have gone better for Dara but unfortunately his father struggled at being a lone parent, as he himself had succumbed to alcohol and gambling addiction.

He came to my class aged nine. He struggled in the traditional classroom setting, particularly with reading and writing. He was very up and down and had daily explosive outbursts, when faced with situations he found challenging. However, I saw that he was very intelligent and streetwise. He could quickly compute calculations in his head and was practical and gifted with his hands. He was a great conversationalist and enjoyed the opportunity to fix, mend or create something new out of discarded items.

Dara displayed the classic fight or flight response. He was quick to answer back to defend his position and could cut you to the quick with a sarcastic comment. He was acutely self-aware of what he didn't have, compared to his classmates. Despite being the *'tough-nut'* on the yard, he was empathetic towards children with special needs or those that struggled with social interaction. He always defended the weakest child.

I gravitated to him straightaway, despite his challenging behaviours. I knew that there was an immense level of hurt inside him. I consulted with the NEPS Psychologist (National Educational Psychological Service) on how best to meet his needs. She simply said, *'he is crying out for help'*. He had previously never opened up to any teacher or psychologist as to the underlying cause of his behaviours. However, she said that she knew from interactions with him, that he trusted me and that perhaps I was the one person he would open up to. Dara craved one to one attention. He was the first person to put up his hand to help. I could rely on him, and he was learning that he could rely on me. When a good level of trust was established between us, I decided that I would take him under my wing. We bonded.

The first thing I did every day, upon meeting him in the school yard, was to greet him and check in to see how his morning had gone. I worked with him one-on-one, for an hour per week. We partook in different activities like cooking, gardening and board games. It was during these interactions, while Dara was focused on something he liked doing and was good at, that he opened up and confided in me about his childhood experiences and how they manifested themselves in his behavioural outbursts. He recounted stories aged three of being locked in a room; of not having anything to eat or watching his mother drink alcohol while he sat in a corner. He had a sense of walls caving in on him, feeling trapped and confined. He was a highly emotionally sensitive child and became overwhelmed quite easily. Particularly when he was in situations where he felt not good enough, compared to others; or where he observed happy family interactions, something Dara never had, but craved.

Dara was one of approximately fifteen students in that group who were struggling because of various sensory needs. I knew that these children were lost in the traditional classroom setting. They weren't achieving, even though they had the capability. As one person once said, *"If children don't learn the way we teach, well then, we must teach the way they learn"*.

I spoke with the principal, and we agreed that I would teach Dara again the following year; along with a number of other children from his year that were finding school difficult for various reasons. My style of teaching changed and I was determined to focus more on the way these children learned. Which was through the practical application of subjects like Maths, English and Geography. Things that really worked included:

- Use of PowerPoint presentations instead of History or Geography books.
- Weekly Science experiments.
- Oral language skills, listening skills and guided reading.
- Maths-trails that involved going to the shop – transacting with money or figuring out time using bus station timetables etc.
- Gardening

- Cooking
- Woodwork

We focused a lot on social stories and related them to life's challenges. The children could identify themes in the story that were particularly relevant to them. They started to learn new mechanisms to cope with some of the issues they faced in their own lives. Scores for all students improved that year in all standardised tests. We, as teachers, got a better understanding of each student's needs and as a result, we could tailor their learning to achieve the best outcome for them. Dara was so proud of himself that he could do as well as others, if not better.

"Tell me and I forget, teach me and I may remember, involve me and I learn".

Dara went on to secondary school. He called back to visit me in Primary School on a few occasions. He confided in me that he ended up in foster care and that it was one of the best things that could have happened to him. He settled in very well with the family. His social care worker kept me updated and I was happy to find out that he was now settled with a farming family. He was a great addition to their home and was highly regarded for his work on the farm and around the house. He completed his Junior Cert and

91

stayed out of trouble. As the years went on, I often wondered where he had ended up. I followed up with his social worker many years later. To my delight, he said that Dara was now working in a job that suited his skillset. His job involves working with the public, making sales, and helping people solve practical problems. The social worker said that Dara often spoke of me to this day. I still speak of Dara to this day. I am so thankful that I got to know Dara and to help him on his life's journey. I hope he knows that he too, helped me on mine.

Stranger Danger

The lesson for me in Dara's story is *'Don't judge a book by its cover'*. However, this is made more complicated by the fact some people are excellent at hiding their true emotions and intentions. Someone could be feeling jealous, hostile, agitated, or hold bad intentions of control, coercion, or cruelty. Yet they present to the world with a happy and sincere demeanour. However, their true energy is still available to the more sensitive among us.

On occasions, sensitive children may be picking up on the negative intention of someone who is wearing an emotional mask. People who lack understanding of what it truly means to be sensitive, will not be aware of why the sensitive child's emotions change when they encounter someone like this. The child may behave in a manner that is not in line with their own experiences. As the true owner of these emotions is cloaking their feelings, the sensitive child will be the only one behaving in an aggressive way. When asked to explain why they are behaving in this manner they will not have an answer. Their negativity is not in proportion to the events of their day. To those who do not have a strong intuition they will not sense the true energy of those in their company. The child, exhibiting a copy of the cloaked energy' is now seen as the one with the anger issues.

Alternatively, the child may become distressed whenever they are asked to be in someone's company. They may refuse to comply with the adults' instructions. They may be *'feeling'* stranger danger but have no evidence to justify this. Other than '*I don't like them*'. We owe it to our children to listen to their fears, as their intuition may in fact be correct. If this was a potential abuser, they are cloaking their intentions. Their true feelings are not obvious in their expression or behaviour. Someone who presents as *'sweetness and light'* may underneath be jealous, manipulative, or even dangerous. The sensitive child will be impacted by the true nature. For those who have never had these experiences it can be hard to comprehend. To the oblivious adult, the child will be the only one acting out.

ELECTRIC SHOCK

Growing up on a farm in the West of Ireland brought freedom and outdoor adventures. Summertime was especially exciting, not least because there was no school. That said, we had the extra chores of cutting and saving hay, weeding vegetables, cutting and stacking turf, and the house got its annual spring clean. Summertime meant more children to play with. We were allowed roam more freely during the summer months, as were the neighbouring children. Added to this there would be an influx of other children. Adults, from the community who had left the countryside to live in cities, frequently left their children in the care of extended family in the countryside, for the summer. Unfortunately, in our changing world this rarely happens anymore.

Our farm was mainly a dairy farm as were all the farms in the area. The fields were frequently divided into strips using an electric fence. The cattle would graze within the strip. Every evening the older children were tasked with moving the electric fence further along the field to allow additional grazing. This may seem like a cruel method of containing cattle but

94

generally, on seeing the wire and stakes the cattle accustomed themselves to grazing in the allocated strip. It also kept any neighbouring cattle from breaking into the herd. Especially any bulls.

As youngsters we were '*initiated*' as were the visiting city children. Older children would make a big show of walking up to the fence and hold it with their right hand. Then another child would take their left hand. The youngest or newest child visiting the farm would be encouraged to take the hand of the second child. Completely unexpectedly they would receive an electric shock. Not enough to do any physical damage. Nevertheless, a very unpleasant experience that probably lasted less than a second. Having observed the older children take hold of the fence we would feel safe and be delighted that the older children were allowing us to play with them. What the younger child was unaware of was that the others were wearing wellingtons with rubber soles which grounded them. They received no shock.

Imagine experiencing a similar shock every time you were in the company of someone who was distressed, annoyed or angry, even if that person was wearing their happy face. Empathic children can experience a similar shock from all those they encounter who are in emotional turmoil. Is it any wonder they occasionally retaliate? Young children may physically hit out or bite others for no apparent reason. But perhaps there is a reason. Perhaps, they are very sensitive. Likewise, children who have limited speech, or are limited by disability may simply be trying to defend themselves from the shock. Or to defend themselves from whom they perceive responsible for the shock. This is not just restricted to when they're in the company of those experiencing anger. It can be any emotional turmoil. If someone is in grief, or extreme anxiety, this can also impact an empathic child in the same way as the electric fence experience. The child who hits out in their efforts to stop the emotional assault - may then be reprimanded for what they perceive as simply defending themselves.

Sensitive people when in the presence of someone who is angry may find themselves impacted in a way that resembles a physical assault. It may feel as if someone has unexpectedly put their hand on the child's chest or stomach and pushed them. The child's internal computer may realise it has taken on a virus and try to combat it. If the sensitive child becomes angry or traumatised by this new emotion, their behaviour will appear irrational. To the observing adult this sudden outburst is without reason, warning, or explanation. The child's adapted response to an unexpected emotional assault may continue throughout their lives.

PREJUDICE

Some sensitive children will sense aggressive personalities. Others may be more impacted by the energy of the person on the receiving end of an angry outburst. The victim may be feeling fear, injustice, sadness, or frustration. This may be the sentiment which the sensitive person absorbs. When I was a child, this is the programme I felt most - with its own consequences. When in this programme, I automatically assumed that the fear, sadness, or injustice I was experiencing was mine. I was frequently the one who stood up to the bully on behalf of others. I spoke for the victim, or I went to care for them. Not surprisingly, this did not go down well with the nuns.

MONKEY SEE, MONKEY DO

My childhood included listening to stories told by my grandparents and grandaunt of injustice by the British soldiers during their occupancy of our country. Relatives from previous generations had taken active roles in defending their people, through participating and aiding guerrilla warfare. There were stories of local towns being burnt to the ground. Older stories were also told, including tales of famine times where my ancestors were evicted for not being able to pay their rent.

When these stories were recalled, they evoked strong emotions in the storytellers. They described atrocities they had witnessed or were told by their parents and neighbours. Following the atrocities there was the hardship endured by the families whose husbands and fathers had been shot or left trapped in burning buildings. Stories of neighbours taking in neighbours. The feelings I absorbed were of the injustice felt; as the well-equipped occupiers took advantage of the weaker, ill equipped and outnumbered rural dwellers. The people telling these stories were people I loved. I felt their pain, and sense of injustice. These were emotions that were familiar to me. These same emotions surfaced frequently in me during my time in school. When my classmates endured unjustifiable abuse at the hands of those charged with our care.

Generally, any time I was in direct communication with the nuns I was switched off. However, when the nun was interacting directly with another child, I often felt safe enough to be emotionally present. I was unprepared for when they received a punishment. With my attention on them, I would soak up their programme. As they became the target of an assault, I absorbed their emotions of pain and fear. I added this onto my own feelings of shock and trauma, from witnessing these scenes. There was also the perceived injustice I felt, due to the preferential treatment some students received from the nuns. Students from small farms and poorer backgrounds were treated much less favourably. Injustice is an emotion that triggers me. Not just when I feel the energy of the victim but also when I am a witness to such events.

It has got me in trouble many times. I have literally stood in front of children who were about to receive corporal punishment. They still got hit, but so did I. Too many times in my life, I have gone to the rescue of others when it was not appropriate to do so. I have become involved in situations that were not mine. At the time, I had no understanding of empathy, and no understanding that much of what I was feeling was not mine. When someone is in trouble it is often more beneficial if we can walk beside them, instead of in front of them. By being a support instead of a hero, the victim learns to fight their own battles, to talk out their problems and come to their own solutions. If we stand in front, we take on the fight. As a child I did not have this knowledge.

Today I feel a very strong sense of injustice when I see how sensitive children are treated. They are frequently perceived as the problem. To a large extent society lacks the understanding of what is involved, the daily struggles and difficulties experienced by this group of people. Awareness is needed. With awareness, perhaps those tasked with the care of these challenged children will make efforts to ensure assistance and strategies are provided.

The emotion of injustice runs deep for most sensitive/empathic people. They often feel a lack of understanding from others, or indeed, no attempt at understanding. In the following story we meet Anna, a gentle and kind little girl who has often experienced feelings of injustice. In school she is frequently singled out and excluded from weekly rewards by her teacher. Her crime is her sensitivity.

WHY?
ELLEN

I never fully understood what the word empath meant until I had my own children. Getting to know my children meant that I got to know myself better. I came to understand my life as an empath.

The moment my second child, Anna, was born and raised up in front of me, I knew that she had a special gift. A carbon-copy of myself; an empath. Anna is a highly sensitive child. She watches my every move and absorbs mine and others' feelings. She easily picks up on energy that is not her own. She notices more in her environment than others do and deeply reflects on all she sees. I needed some help to learn more about how to parent an empathic child.

I read Bríd's first book '*Memories and Missions*' and immediately knew that she could help. My first encounter with Bríd was when she did a healing for Anna when she was a toddler. Anna had difficulty sleeping and woke very early every morning. I know now that she was tuning into the world and picking up on energy that was not her own. Within days of the treatment Anna settled. It was reassuring to know that Bríd could read our daughter so well and help with how she was feeling, even as a toddler.

When I was growing up, I knew that how I was feeling inside was different. I could pick up on how people were feeling and sometimes feel heat or pain from encounters with others. I felt drained regularly after certain interactions. I always felt drawn to equality and a sense of justice. I began to notice these traits in Anna as she started to grow and develop her own personality.

Anna's true nature as an empath really shone out when she started Montessori. By meeting other children and teachers she was encountering different energies, unlike those she was familiar with at home. She would talk for days about something that she saw as unfair; if a child was mean or if her friends did not sit with her. She would bring up a certain incident, weeks or even months later and retell the story in detail. Bríd was called on and always gave great advice about how to work with Anna and help her disconnect from the energy of others. As Anna was small at the time, we had strategies like blowing a bubble off our hand to blow away those worries.

When she started primary school and she became more independent in her learning and thinking, things came to light about how adults could have a negative impact on Anna as an empath. Her teacher was the only Junior Infants teacher in this country school. She had her way of teaching and had high standards. Anna is a capable child and is eager to learn. We did not have concerns about her academic ability, but I was very concerned about her emotionally after some incidents in the school year.

Anna never really hit it off with her teacher. There was one incident when Anna was not allowed to partake in a singing routine in class. Anna saw this as being unfair and she cried every evening about it after.

On another occasion, Anna was told that she would not get the sweet at the end of the week as she had cried when she got something wrong in an exercise. In the eyes of a five-year-old the weekly sweet is the ultimate goal! She felt she was being punished for her feelings and she could not understand the reasons behind it.

We were told at the Parent Teacher evening that crying was our daughter's 'fall back' when things did not work out. We have a five-year-old child who is highly sensitive and a grown adult who did not understand that she was punishing a child for being emotional. Anna was told that "you'll be in senior infants next year and you can't be crying like that". Sadly, feelings were never spoken about in this school.

As a mother, I carried the guilt that I doubted my child for some time during the school year. I asked so many questions: Was my child misbehaving, was she breaking the rules, was she behaving badly in class? But Anna was so upset in the evenings and often mentioned that she had tummy aches, I knew there was more. Other parents were aware of what was happening, as their own children brought stories home of Anna's distress.

I knew I had to chat to Bríd and immediately she put my mind at ease. She knew Anna's energy and we talked about Anna's sensitive nature and how the lack of fairness was bothering her. Bríd knew that the energy of others was affecting Anna and we teased out how we could help her.

Bríd guided us to do practical activities with Anna at home to keep her grounded. We explained to her that God gave her a special heart and she feels things on a much deeper level than others do. She likes swimming and we encouraged her to let go of anything that she is not happy about when in the water. Bríd had strategies like asking Anna to put the feeling into her pocket until she got home and then asking the fairies to take it away. With her new strategies she is now able to cope when feeling upset at school. Anna is very relaxed in her home environment. She does not cry when things go wrong. She is a happy child and is kind and caring to her family.

As an empath Anna is solely interested in fairness and justice. Everyone should get their turn. Everyone should get a second chance to make amends. Everyone should get help or understanding from an adult and talk things through if there is a problem. While I'm grateful for the academic start that Anna was given by her teachers, I'm a little bewildered by the system. In fact, I work with young people myself but in a setting where we encourage our students to talk to an adult when they need help, when they're down or have a problem. If a student is upset, we do our best to support them. Every single child that sits before me has a different make up, a different story and a different energy. We are not all the same. Sadly, Anna did not get that support from the adults in the classroom this year but as her parents we will carry on with strategies that support her as an empath. We are very grateful to Bríd for enriching us with these strategies to help our little girl.

For many sensitive children when faced with difficult situations, they generally switch off. Most are likely to cry more often than less sensitive children. But considering they are feeling more emotional pain than others; then this response is perfectly understandable. One woman compared herself to an aardvark. *"I'm just like an anteater. I've spent my life hoovering up everyone else's sadness and pain".* Being on the upper side of the builder's spirit level means being much more compassionate. Therefore, these children will be emotional on hearing sad stories or watching traumatic events. They then add to their own feelings, a copy of the sadness experienced by others. During emotionally charged events these children will soak or hover up copies of others sharing the experience. Sadly, much of today's society does not allow for this response. These children are frequently teased for how much they cry, while it's their bodies' way of coping and attempting to regulate. They are attempting to cry out the virus which is attacking their internal computer.

If we take the example of the sad passing of a beloved granny, the child will be distressed. Hopefully, this is the first time they have experienced loss. In their family environment they have their little hearts open as they are accustomed to the everyday energy in that environment. Now they are soaking up their mum's or dad's sorrow. They are also taking on copies of the sadness their siblings are experiencing. At the funeral service the pain of all those who cared about granny will be experienced by the child. They will be overwhelmed and, yes - if they are switched on, they will need to cry in proportion to all the sadness they have absorbed. Over the coming days and months, this child will unexpectedly pick up on grief of other family members who are triggered by memories of granny. The copies continue to mount up.

Likewise, in daily life, other children in any classroom setting will be experiencing life challenges. As will teachers, classroom assistants, parents, and caregivers. All this emotional pain is available to the aardvark. If the child who has remained open to experiencing emotion, is then teased about how much they are crying, they may have to ditch their coping technique. This limits their options to less healthy ones, including shutting down or removing themselves from the other children.

Prejudices is defined as: *"An unfair and unreasonable opinion or feeling, especially when formed without enough thought or knowledge"*.

Recently, I received a text message from a mother of a seven-year-old sensitive boy. The child is performing well academically at school. His year-end report shows average to above average grades in each subject. Underneath the grades section on the report sheet is a comment box for the teacher. Instead of any compliment on the child's achievements, his report reads: *"Not in control of his emotions"* and *"he cries too much"*. Needless to say, the mum was devastated that all her son's positive strengths and qualities were overlooked. Her child's *'crime'* is that he is sensitive. I reassured the mum that she has a wonderful son, intelligent, smart and caring, with a beautiful heart. Unfortunately, his teacher has no understanding of what it means to be sensitive. Telling someone they shouldn't be who they are, is not going to change them, or help them. It is similar to requiring someone to change their eye colour. It can, however, have a negative impact on their self-esteem, and self-confidence. Those responsible for the care of these young people, owe it to them, and indeed to every child, to come to an understanding of their individuality, and encourage them to flourish.

Moving from primary to secondary school will present further challenges and adjustments for every child. New subjects are added to their curriculum, new rules, longer hours, new teachers, extra homework, peer pressure, all this while their own bodies are changing from child to adult. For the sensitive child, participating in a classroom of hormonal teenagers can leave them feeling overwhelmed. Adding all these adjustments to their personal challenges can seem insurmountable.

Many children overwhelmed in their school settings would truly love to be allowed stay at home. In more recent years, teenagers who find themselves overwhelmed are starting to take a stand and refuse to participate in society. Without healthy tools, many will drop out of the educational system. They will not reach their potential. I have met many teenagers who have done just that. They could manage academically but the other transitions proved too much.

Katie, a nineteen-year-old, spoke of how she literally could not get past the school gate. Feelings of fear and nausea overtook her. Some mornings she managed to get out of the car and walk as far as the gate; other mornings she could not force herself to open the car door. In the end, she found it difficult to leave her home. She finished her education through home schooling and got her grades but felt she would not be able to cope with the stress of attending college. It is so sad, when a teenager feels they cannot cope in the mainstream education system because they are overwhelmed, and the supports needed are not available. Until such time as they develop tools and a new understanding of their sensitivity, sadly, dropping out may be the only safe option available for these teenagers.

Declan, a sixteen-year-old student, came to see me with his father. He explained how he could manage some subjects but felt completely overwhelmed in certain classes. On talking it through, he came to the realisation that the classes he struggled with the most included a girl who seemed very troubled. Declan could simply not be in the company of this girl.

Both Katie and Declan had experienced varying levels of understanding and levels of stigma from their peers and teachers. During my conversations with both these students I was able to explain about their sensitivity and give them simple tools they could use in their daily lives to stay grounded. I also gave them tools (discussed in later chapters) for when they needed to disconnect from the energy of others. Following these conversations, they were better equipped to participate in the social arena of their everyday lives.

THE PEOPLE-PLEASER

From early childhood the sensitive child is aware of their surroundings, and the emotions of those with whom they share these surroundings. Those born to hardworking, burdened, ill, exhausted, anxious, insecure, frustrated or depressed parents will feel their struggle. They will have a much stronger awareness of the family undercurrents than their siblings and parents, who are less sensitive. With this awareness, they generally take it upon themselves to lighten the load. Frequently this child will sacrifice play and light-heartedness, and instead takes on chores and responsibilities beyond their years. This becomes their everyday pattern.

- *"Are you ok?"*
- *"What can I get you?"*
- *"Can I help?"*
- *"Don't mind me".*
- *"I'm fine".*
- *"I don't need anything".*
- *"I don't mind".*
- *"As long as you are ok, I'm ok".*

111

They learn to function by putting the needs of those in turmoil first. If they can lessen the distress of their loved ones, this will greatly reduce their own distress on two levels. Firstly, by helping those who are struggling, the energy in their home will feel better. Thus, reducing the impact on a sensory level. Secondly, as a caring child they, themselves, want the needs of others to be met. Especially when those needs are of those they care about most. When the cause of the adults' emotional turmoil is a one-off event, the child's intervention may be sufficient to make the changes necessary and save the day.

Unfortunately, more often than not, these struggles will have existed for some time, possibly before the child was even born. No matter how much they sacrifice or prioritise the needs of others, they will not be able to fix their parents' struggles. They may provide short-term reprieves, while lessening the load; perhaps by minding younger siblings or doing extra chores. But the situation will possibly be repeated daily and may be beyond repair. The adults can come to depend on the child, to continue being their solution. The child accepts the *"well done"*, *"good girl/boy"*, *"I'd be lost without you"* while feeling the gratitude of the adult. This becomes a way of life, help others, put them first, problem solve for someone else. Then be rewarded with some words of gratitude while feeling the burden lessen briefly.

The people-pleaser is very slow to say *"NO"* to anyone and tends to lack the ability to have safe boundaries. They have become accustomed to fixing things for others, leaving their own needs to last. Perhaps they never identify their own needs. Typically, around the age of two we start to work out our likes and dislikes. We begin expressing our needs. We will all have witnessed the temper tantrums of children going through *'the terrible two's'*. *"Me, me, me, mine, me want, no"*. But this is in fact a very necessary life skill that is being learnt. The toddler is learning to identify their needs, their likes and dislikes. They are working out their boundaries and expressing their needs. The two-year-old has not mastered these skills, and so their response is louder or more exaggerated or dramatic than necessary. As they grow, they learn to share, to work out what they will and won't accept and how to adjust their needs within society. They learn to balance their needs with those in their environment and what others will accept and expect from them.

Unfortunately, the people-pleaser has not learnt this skill. When asked a question of choice they will often answer with *"I don't mind"*. If asked by their parent, *"Which lolly pop would you like?"* They answer with *"I don't mind"*. Whereas other children will generally have no problem stating their preference. *"I want the green one"* or *"I want the strawberry flavour"*. The adult will now assume this is the preference of all the children. One child prefers green, one prefers strawberry and the other child is happy with the remainder. Every time there are lolly pops on offer, the sensitive child will now get the third preference. Everyone is happy. Or so it seems, but this is not the actual preference of the sensitive child. They feel the satisfaction of the other children and the satisfaction of the parent, rather than expressing their preference and having their needs met.

When this scenario, and similar scenarios are replayed repeatedly, the sensitive child can eventually become resentful. This is more evident, on the rare occasions, where they are strongly grounded in their own emotions. When they are no longer in people-pleaser mode, they observe their siblings always getting the better-quality gift. They forget they were included in the original conversation of preferences. They forget they have always answered with *"I don't mind"*. The consequence of originally being unable to offer their choice and opinion, is that others grow accustomed to a certain status quo within the group. They get used to their needs being expressed, and met, and to the people-pleaser complying with this pattern.

114

Because the people-pleaser child is not voicing their needs, the focus of the adult can be drawn to the child who is loudly shouting their individual wishes. *"Anything for a peaceful life"*. The quiet child is not complaining and is going along with the suggestions of the adult and the child with the strongest voice, their own needs are often over-looked. When they are asked their preference, they simply do not know. They have spent much of their life speaking as a **WE**. *"Where will we go?"* *"What will we watch?"* *"What will we play?"* As this becomes the norm in their home, play will be dictated by others and the sensitive child will just be grateful to be included. This child needs to be encouraged to be an **I**. To start identifying their likes and dislikes, to gain a better understanding of themselves.

The following testimonial was sent in by Grainne, a wonderful play therapist. She has identified that some children who live as people-pleasers may need encouragement with this skill. After a while the results are truly worth the effort. The example she has sent in was not based on the child's sensitivity. However, it gives a lovely example of how children can be encouraged to discover their likes and dislikes. By doing so they begin to find their voice and begin to find themselves.

PLAY TIME
GRAINNE NAUGHTON

In my work, my learning has always been influenced by the children I have worked with and the way in which they cope in whatever circumstances they are living through. The following tells of one such child.

James is five years old and is struggling with his parents' separation in the last six months. James has a very good relationship with both his mum and dad. Dad has moved out and James is finding it hard to get used to this new arrangement. He does not see his dad as often as he would like, and he especially misses his dad at bedtime. James does not feel like talking about how he is feeling, as it makes him feel sad. In the first few sessions I allow James to take ownership of the therapy space.

In this place he has access to paint, building blocks, sand box, figurines and an assortment of other toys. Initially James flits from toy to sand box finding a sense of what he wants to do and what he does not want to do. He spends time playing with the sand box, adding in glitter in a myriad of colours. He finds figurines and with these he creates a story, which he narrates out loud. In this way, James is igniting his imagination. Through play he is on a journey, that he has created and, where he has free reign to explore without interruption or direction.

Over the weeks James moves between using sand to building toy brick houses, etc., creating stories as he goes. In this way of playing James can imagine a world where he is the author and he is the director of how things are. In his home environment things have changed and are changing at a rate that James finds difficult to understand. For James, having a place to go where he is free to express how he is feeling is important.

The Buffer

Children can often act as a *'buffer'* between an adult and another child. Unfortunately, when the other child is being corrected, the buffer can be seen as the problem in the eyes of others. In their desire to protect the vulnerable, the sensitive child speaks on behalf of someone else, usually without consultation.

END OF YEAR

I remember times in my childhood when I tried to defend other children. There were occasions where I stood in front of children when they were being reprimanded. In hindsight this did not do them, or me, any good.

Our school was a country school, with two classes in each room, junior and senior infants, first and second class, third and fourth class and fifth with sixth class. At the end of each school year, the principal would go from classroom to classroom and call the names of those who were moving up to the next year. As she called the names of the children to move on, they would stand and move to their new designated seating area. Anyone she didn't call, remained in their seat and would have to repeat the year.

At the end of the academic year, when I was in fifth-class, the principal began calling out the names of our class who were moving up to sixth-class. As each name was called, we stood, took our belongings and moved to the sixth-class area of the room. She called all but one name. One girl was left sitting on her own in the fifth-class area. The child sat there and smiled at the nun. But I could feel my heart break, I felt such sadness and injustice. Today I understand that some of this was mine, but I was also putting a copy of the girl's feelings in on top of my own. That day, I left my newly designated seat and walked back and sat with the child who had been left behind. The nun laughed at me and walked out of the classroom to transfer up all the other classes. While she was gone no one spoke, as they knew they would have to witness the beating I was likely to receive.

Protecting someone is admirable if their life is in danger, or if we are tasked with their care. But when it is not our fight and serves no purpose, except to perhaps prolong the event, it is of no benefit. Unfortunately, feeling the distress of another, the sensitive child can step in, attempting to form a buffer between the aggressor and the victim.

Middle Management

On other occasions in their efforts to keep the '*grown ups*' happy, the people-pleaser can step into '*middle management*'. They implement the instructions of the adult; directing the other children to behave in a way they believe the adult desires. Correcting the younger children and enforcing what they believe are the wishes of the adult. All this pressure they take on themselves, believing the adult will be happy and therefore the lives of the other children will be better.

This is a difficult and lonely place for the sensitive child. They are not on equal footing with the adults but are enforcing their wishes or perceived wishes, neither are they a part of the other children's team. They stand alone as they have chosen to behave like '*mini adults*' in their desire to keep others happy and safe. They sense when the adults are annoyed,

119

fatigued, or frustrated, and take it upon themselves to make everything better. This is an impossible task, as no one can always be happy.

Some will step into middle management not out of love and concern for the adults but instead out of fear. If they are unfortunate to have a parent with violent tendencies, lacking tolerance, perhaps with addiction problems or with narcissistic or psychopathic tendencies, they will endeavour to protect whoever is in danger. They sense the undercurrents and attempt to pacify the aggressor by trying to meet their needs. Again, this comes with a high price tag.

- If they are covering up someone else's behaviour, then the *'red flags'* may not be so obvious to the outside world and the violent behaviour goes unnoticed.
- If they are standing between the aggressor and shielding younger siblings, those they protected will not be aware of the risk from the aggressor. These children will form their opinions of the parent/carer based on their own shielded experiences and will have a completely different outlook to their 'middle management' sibling.
- If they are standing between their parents, shielding one from the other they may be cushioning the victim to a point where they

delay making decisions to make necessary changes.

Whatever the scenario, each carries a hefty price tag. The following story details the life of a young girl. She grew up in a one parent family, where unfortunately, that parent was a physically abusive alcoholic. Being sensitive to their needs, the girl acted as the buffer between her mother and her young siblings. Because of her sacrifices the younger children were not aware of much of what their sister experienced and in time she paid the ultimate price.

THE PROTECTOR
LAURA

Childhood for me consists mainly of memories of looking after my younger sisters, always cooking with whatever foods I could find. Or baking anything edible, with any flour and whatever else would moisten it to give them a treat for school. My mother drank endlessly and there was never food in the house. Some of the local nuns were so kind and used to give us lots of treats. I always tried to hide from my younger siblings how little was available. They never realised and still don't.

At night I would have to sit with my mother, just speaking softly through the darkness so she could sleep. If she woke, I would have to cross dark fields at three or four o clock to knock on pub doors for alcohol. They usually didn't answer. It was easier to wait in the darkness of the fields than go home empty handed and be beaten to a pulp. The younger children stayed in bed and slept while I sat singing to her.

Even though she drank constantly I always convinced myself I wanted to be a maid when I grew up. I would clean for her and do all the housework trying to please her, just wanting to be validated and wanted. Often when I was with the nuns or speaking with neighbours, I would try to find the courage to tell them the truth of what was happening at home. Once I did tell a neighbour, Rita, a little of my story. She arrived at the house and tried to see what was going on. Though she saw the bruises on all of us children and how underweight we were, my mother convinced her she was a great mother. As Rita left, she said to me *"You are blessed to have a mother like her"*. My heart sank.

My mother realised I had told Rita her secrets. When our neighbour left, I got absolutely killed, I was even punched with an iron bar. She held the poker in the fire till it went red and then brought it right up to

122

my face to let me feel the heat. I know that people heard my screams on different occasions, but no one tried to help.

Shortly after the visit from our neighbour, I returned from school one day to find the house empty. My mother had taken my sisters out of school early and had packed their bags and left. There was no note, or address or explanation left. They had just gone. I had been left behind. Despite the fact I had worked so hard to please her. I had done everything in the house, practically rearing my siblings and sitting up with her at night when she was afraid of her demons, she had left me behind.

I was taken into foster care. Later I discovered they had moved county, to live with relatives in Carlow. My main concern was for my sisters and not for my sadness at being abandoned. I believed they needed protection, so I wrote to them every week. I got a job in a local hotel, cleaning bedrooms and washing dishes and sent them my earnings.

Up until my mother's death, I still tried to gain her love and acknowledgement. I believed I had done wrong and needed to make amends. Unfortunately, no matter how hard I tried, this love was never forthcoming. My sisters are now adults. Neither one realises the childhood I had. Instead, they treat me like the black sheep of the family and can be very hurtful in their comments. By making the decision to protect them I got left behind by my mother. Now my younger sisters also choose to leave me behind.

When a child steps into middle management they step out of childhood. They sacrifice their playtime, and natural childhood interactions with other children. On the occasions when they do play, it tends to be games that are age appropriate, safe, or educational for their younger siblings. They play in a supervisory capacity. The younger siblings tend to team up together excluding the middle management, who they do not perceive as their equal. The child who takes on this role is not always the eldest, and this brings further complications. Older children will not take kindly to being '*bossed*' by a younger sibling.

In the following testimonial we get a glimpse into the life of a family with generations of people-pleasers and buffers. Aoife tells of her grandfather's inability, to meet the needs of his family. His son (her father) also took on the role of the people-pleaser and married a strong and sometimes dominant partner. He tried to pacify her but ultimately, he was unable to stand up to her behaviour. Aoife, herself sensitive, was aware of the struggles of her dad and she attempted to step into middle management between her mother and her siblings. Later in her own marriage she drifted from people-pleaser to middle management between her husband and their children. Aoife is now learning her own value and allowing others to do the same.

FAMILY PATTERNS
AOIFE B.

I always wanted to be a mother. The thought of having my own children and raising them was just Heaven to me. Every part of my being cried out for motherhood. The years of having my youngsters around me and all the joy of sharing my excitement at the world with them was a glorious time. Sadly, on occasion, these beautiful days were plagued by their dad's behaviour. After we finally separated, he wanted revenge; revenge as he believed I was taking his children away from him and revenge for rejecting him. I now understand he is a man who used emotional abuse and occasional violent tendencies to ease his own pain and feelings of lack of self-worth.

When he had access to the children, he found a way to encourage them to find fault in and become indifferent towards their mother. He did this particularly with our son whose confusion led to poor boundaries and toxic behaviour often through defiance and rudeness. At times, my own boundaries were pushed and I found disciplining my son a challenge.

The younger of the two children, my daughter and I managed to find happiness. Despite my son at ten not being returned to me after visitation with his dad. The separation from my son was devastating to us all. Despite this my daughter and I had a very natural bond and she was a true salvation. Until eventually at thirteen she too was influenced by her dad to go live with him.

My own childhood had been one of happiness and I progressed with ease through my formative years and I largely have quite happy memories. My parents were very cultured and educated people who both worked long hours, my mother more so than my father. She was more demonstrative than my father who was the agreeable and often the pacifier in the relationship. I was the youngest of four children.

I remember always wishing that my father would stand up to my mother's sometimes overly critical outbursts. Both my parents were products of parents who found it difficult to show them love and both shared the absence of a father figure in their lives. I felt I was always having to compensate for any unmet emotional needs. On some level I resented this later in life and swore I would never repeat the pattern with my own children.

My father had lost his father to suicide at the age of fourteen (which my father never disclosed to me). My mother's alcoholic father left the family for another woman. I never knew my paternal grandfather, but I found out that he worked long days in a small corner grocery shop to provide for his family and in the evenings encouraged the proletariat to fight for workers' rights. Often speaking out in front of large groups. As a Polish Jewish immigrant in America in the 1930s, whose remaining family in Poland perished in the Holocaust, he struggled to make a living. When faced with anti-Semitic discrimination and in turn experiencing his corner shop being robbed several times, he, as a very proud man, could not face being unable to provide for his family. He chose to end it all at the base of a noose.

When I met Bríd for the first time she sensed that I had been a people-pleaser in the family household and had often held a middle-management type role, trying to keep everyone happy. Thinking back to those days, I realised I was never asked what I felt or what I wanted. The older siblings tended to take centre stage and I spent my time looking up to them, in search of a role model of a kind that never materialised. I just went along with what the family wanted. I remember being polite and always respectful to my parents, even while navigating the turbulent teenage years. But then I can remember wanting to break away so badly and find my own way, which I imagine was what most young people want to do.

However, my formative years shaped me in a way that I never imagined. I remember resenting my dad for a perceived *'weakness'*. I concentrated very little on his kind and attentive nature and more on my perceptions. I desperately wanted him to stand up to my often unrestrained, domineering mother. Although she offered love and kindness in abundance; she struggled very much with her own self-esteem and identity. Unfortunately, this often came out in outbursts, which stemmed back to her own very detached mother and a largely absent, abusive, alcoholic father. I think this led to my fear of expressing my own needs and I struggled to be assertive throughout my life. A trait my mother often questioned with amazement. Maybe because she overcame adversity with strength. This was not something I would acquire until much later in my own life.

When it came to choosing relationships, Bríd recognised that the reason for so many failed relationships was due to choosing men whose needs I thought I could meet. Rather than seeing them as my equal. I perceived being the *'saviour'* in the partnership rather than choosing people for the type of person they were. Perhaps when I look back, I felt that everyone seemed to be finding love and I was being left behind. I would attract a certain type of renegade, those defying convention, which seemed to thrill me but of course those type of relationships offered little stability and emotional security.

Even when I was in my forties, I initially believed I met the right person, who offered stability and made me feel a little more visible. But he himself lacked a sense of self-worth and ran away from the world and me. He often immersed himself in the fantasy of gaming when life got tough. Eventually I lost my daughter to him. She, like my son, was encouraged by her dad to isolate herself from me. Our relationship broke down under the strain. I realised I could not fix my husband, my son or my daughter or anyone else, as I couldn't fix myself. For the first time I realised that it was not always up to me to fix and compensate. When did I stop thinking that my needs mattered? It felt like I had done a lifetime of this. I realised it was a pattern of behaviour I had taken as the norm since my childhood.

I reluctantly left my children in England with their father, they were then aged thirteen and fifteen. I escaped to Ireland from their toxic and hostile projections onto their mother. This was an attitude perpetuated in their new home life. My children had accepted it as the norm. I felt a tremendous loss that crippled me. Losing my son had nearly killed me. But then losing my daughter to the man who had previously stolen my son from me, and then callously encouraged my daughter to do the same, left me with little reason to go on. Bríd recognised that if I had stayed in England, I would have suffered great depression and like my grandad I had considered ending my life. She was right.

I returned to the only place I knew would heal me and that was in Ireland, where I had grown up. It was at this point in my session with Bríd that she sensed my grandfather's spirit with me. She had said that my grandfather had been relieved that I hadn't taken the course of action that he had, and that I had held on. That threatened or diminished role of the parent, as provider, was something my grandfather understood and he knew in time I would find my way back to my children.

I had turned to Bríd when I found it difficult to face the decisions and actions I had taken and had been unable to forgive myself. She spoke to me about the importance of saving ourselves. Thus, enabling me to carry tremendous love and openness to receive the love of my children when they were ready. She explained I had provided my children with important life lessons, particularly my daughter. I realised my actions had shown the example that when we find ourselves in desperately unhealthy situations, it is important that we do not suffer in silence and stay. We need to break away and heal ourselves and learn to embrace self-preservation, only then can we fulfil our intended role.

My teenager children will not see this now, but maybe they will come to see the situation as an important path for them to take towards finding themselves.

When we live our lives as people-pleasers, inevitably disillusion and frustration set in. I compare the emotional heart to the human heart. The physical heart receives the blood supply through the veins and then pumps blood out to the body through the arteries. Blood in, blood out. Both are equally important. Both need to be working in tandem. It is the same with our emotional hearts. It is essential that as we pump out love and kindness to others, love and kindness are returned.

I explain to my clients there are three ways to fill our emotional cup. The first is by giving to others. If we picture a little girl picking daisies for her mum. As she runs to hand the gift to her parent she is beaming with joy. *"Look what I got you"*. As she hands over her precious treasure, the child is full of happiness at being able to gift someone she cares about. Through the act of giving, she is filling her emotional cup.

The second way we fill our cup is by learning to meet our own needs. In the earlier story, submitted by Grainne Naughton, we saw James identifying what he wanted to do. He learnt how to make these decisions without guidance from anyone else. As he walked around the therapy room, he sampled the options available and gave himself permission to identify the option that suited his needs best on each occasion. As we learn to address our own needs, we are not dependent on others to do so. Therefore, we are less vulnerable and more likely to start practicing safe boundaries.

The third option is by allowing others to gift us. For the people-pleaser it can be very hard to accept kindness, gifts or even complements. Frequently the people-pleaser does not see their own worth and yet can see the value of others and their achievements. They do not want to be a burden. For them the needs of others come first. When someone does compliment them, they are unable to accept and often reply with a personal put down. *"That's a lovely top"*. *"Oh, this old thing, I've had it for years, I got it on sale"*. They are unable to accept the gift with a genuine *"thank you"*. I explain to the people-pleasers if they are unable to accept gestures of appreciation it is similar to the mum telling the little girl *"You shouldn't have, I didn't want them, I don't need them"*. I explain it is unkind to reject appropriate tokens and gestures of love and appreciation. The person gifting us with the token is filling their cup when we learn to graciously accept.

If we keep telling our friends we are *"fine, don't mind me, as long as you are ok, I'm ok"* eventually the heart will run dry. The person who started out trying to please everyone may end up feeling unappreciated or victimised. We can turn against the people we initially set out to please. In school I eventually worked out that, no matter how hard I tried, I was never going to please or impress those tasked with my education.

The nuns at my school were unable to see the value and uniqueness of the individual. Their values seemed to be based more by social status and academic ability. I remember finally accepting this when I was in sixth class.

CHRISTMAS GIFTS

Before the Christmas holidays, our teacher explained how many families in Ireland were not financially able to buy Christmas presents for their children. She asked us to bring in any spare toys we had at home. She said she was not asking that our parents buy anything new, but if there were any toys in good condition we no longer used, these would be perfect. She continued by adding another condition. We were told that we were the fortunate ones, many were not as fortunate as us. Therefore, to show our appreciation to God for all that we did have, we should give a toy we had a particular personal value in.

I grew up as one of eight children on a small dairy farm in the West of Ireland, where the land was poor, and farming was difficult. My parents had provided for us as best they possibly could, and Santa had always left lovely gifts. That said, by age eleven I had very few toys and even fewer that I had any attachment to. I did however have one doll that I loved. I had owned her for several years, and I used to confide in her about the painful experiences from school and my various challenges in life. I have always held strong religious beliefs; I may not have been good at reciting catechism in school, but I really believed (and still believe) in God. If God wanted me to give a toy that was important to me to someone less fortunate for Christmas, then it had to be my doll, Lizzy.

The following morning, I brushed Lizzy's hair and explained to her what was happening. I sadly and yet proudly placed her in the box on the nun's desk. One child brought in several new board games and jigsaws, all still in their wrappings. The nun singled out this child and all her wonderful gifts. Mine with many others were discarded. I spent the day trying to work out a way to get Lizzy back but unfortunately an opportunity did not present itself. From that day on I stopped trying to please the nun. For me she had lied to us. She was a nun and she had lied. She had given us this big lecture on the importance of personal sacrifice. Now she was singling out someone who had done the opposite. I had believed her and had given her my precious Lizzy, which she had no value in.

Looking back with today's understanding, I realise I had stayed switched on that morning because I had Lizzy with me, and therefore I felt such pain. I also realise that emotionally I was not as mature as many of my peers. Having been switched off for so much of school, I still played with my doll and was quite childish in much of my behaviour. From that day on my opinion of this nun must have been obvious as her distain for me also seemed to grow. From that incident, I no longer made eye contact with her and was even more withdrawn than previously.

I used to travel to and from school on the school bus. The primary bus passed by the gate to our farm and all I had to do was walk the two hundred yards to the house. On the way home, I always looked after the younger children. Making sure they had their coats and walked with them from the school to the car park to get the bus home. The bus collected us at 3pm, even though school did not officially finish till 3pm. This meant we had to leave the classroom by 2.50pm to be on time. Shortly after the incident with Lizzy, the nun informed me that I was no longer allowed leave the classroom early. I now had to wait for the end of class at 3pm. This meant I would miss the bus. The driver had another school run to do after ours and would not wait ten minutes for just one child.

I was the only child from that school run who wasn't on the bus. The solution my parents devised was for me to travel home on the secondary school bus. This left the town at 4.30pm and so for an hour and a half I had to wait. Thankfully one of the children from the town invited me to wait at her home and her mum couldn't have been nicer to me. This solved the first part of the problem. The bus driver for the secondary school was less than impressed to be taking me, but reluctantly agreed. This was all of forty-five years ago, before the mandatory seat belts or health and safety rules on numbers. The bus was seriously overcrowded with children standing in the passageway and many sitting three, instead of two, in the seats. This was my idea of hell.

At the time, most secondary schools were segregated whereby the boys attended the monastery and girls attended the convent. At 4.30 pm these hormonal teenagers were packed physically in together, up close and personal. I was completely overwhelmed by all their energy. Some of the older boys were not nice to me. Being the youngest, smallest, and quietest - I was easy prey. The secondary school bus also took a different route to the primary bus. Instead of being dropped at the gate to our farm, I was dropped about a half mile from home.

My school day went from six hours to eight hours and all because of a nun's power tripping over a little girl with no voice. If I had disliked her before

Christmas, I now held her in complete contempt. I had gone from attempting to please all adults to anger, rejection, sadness, and lack of respect. My heart was in danger of running dry. Fortunately, because of her behaviour, I started learning how to accept generosity and protection. My classmate's mum could not have been kinder in her hospitality, as I waited the hour and a half for the bus. Once on the bus some of the older girls looked out for me, inviting me to sit on their lap or stand beside them in the passageway.

The following September I was delighted, relieved and a bit anxious about starting secondary school. I got used to my classmates and worked out when it was safe to switch on, and which subjects to switch off for. I went back into people-pleaser mode. Unfortunately, some of my new teachers were not pleased with my performance. As mentioned previously I am dyslexic, a word that was not in the general domain at that time. Often my teachers, irrespective of the subject, took it upon themselves to highlight my spelling errors and word reversals. The English teacher decided I was not intelligent enough to be in her classroom and instructed me to join the remedial group. For the remainder of the school year, we sat for English period repeating sentences including *"The cat sat on the mat"*. Second year, thankfully, I had a different English teacher and was allowed participate in her class. I continued to study and do the best I could. I especially liked the logical subjects, maths, science, home economics and geography. These made sense, and I could immerse myself in the solutions, feeling completely grounded while doing so.

That summer we sat our Group Certificate. I got high honours in all my subjects (except art). Those tasked with the correction of my papers had graded me on the content of my answers as opposed to the spelling. I was so delighted and thought finally these people will see me and know there is nothing wrong with my intellect and realise I really was putting in the effort. Wrong. My English teacher from first year approached me in the hallway after the results came in. She asked, *"How did you do it?"* I smiled thinking this was a compliment, it wasn't. *"How did you manage to cheat in every subject?"*

That was the end of my people-pleasing school days but to my detriment. I stopped studying, doing the absolute minimum for homework, just enough to stay out of trouble. This limited my options for both further education and career choices. I had hoped these people would see me, would understand me, and would approve of me. Thankfully I now see myself, I understand myself and I approve of myself,

139

but what a price to pay. With hindsight I realise the teachers of the day were not knowledgeable about dyslexia or many other labels and unfortunately to this day so many are still not knowledgeable about sensitivity and empathy.

THE CHILD'S TOOLBOX

In '*normal*' development, children mirror what they see in everyday life. This is how they grow and learn how to participate in society. They learn how to sit, to walk, to speak, to play, and to develop their social skills from observing and imitating the people in their lives. They also copy their heroes. They pretend to be driving cars or role playing with their dolls and teddies. If they have a particular interest, they may be gifted with miniature versions of a nurses or doctor's uniform, with stethoscope and thermometer. Perhaps they want to be a farmer and will play with toy tractors and plastic farm animals. Others will play house with their toy cooker, teacups and plastic kitchen implements. Some will play shop with a miniature till and fake money. If they want to be a builder, their tool-belt may contain a plastic hammer, drill, and saw. They are copying and learning from their observations from what is available to them, and the explanations provided.

For the sensitive child there are very few healthy examples to follow for regulating their emotions. Sadly, what explanations are given are rarely positive. The child is left to invent their own tools to use. They must create their own toolbox. This can have varying degrees of success. As discussed in the chapter 'Switching Off', many will use this as their main 'go to' tool. They will observe others rather than participating. Some children will invent unique tools.

When learning any skill, we must start with the basic concept. With practice, and determination we master our trade. When learning maths, we do not start with long division or equations. Before learning how to write the numbers one to ten we must first learn how to hold a pencil and write between the lines. We then progress onto addition, subtraction and so on. Similarly, for these children they must start at the beginning.

MOTHER AND DAUGHTER
T. ROSEINGRAVE

Sensitive Definition: "*Quick to detect or respond to slight changes, signals, or influences.*
Having or displaying a quick and delicate appreciation of others' feelings".

Sensitive - a word that only now, in my forties, isn't triggering anymore. A description that only made true sense when I had my own children. When I reflect on my childhood, my sensitive nature was one that was characterised more as an Achilles heel by those close to me. *"There she goes again".* I was commonly referred to as *'Tiny Tears'*.

I could never articulate then how I felt and as I got older and to this day, I am commonly known for saying *"I have a feeling about that"*. With the help of some fabulous therapists in my early thirties, I began to understand what I felt was energy. I am sensitive to the energy of others. I don't hold anyone responsible for not understanding this when I was a child; but today we have a responsibility to understand, learn and enable our little sensitive ones so they can navigate, be heard but more importantly be helped. It is important that they be given a toolbox for life.

My whole life I felt other people's pain, nervousness, or anxiousness. A lot of the time it made me feel like I carried a huge weight on my shoulders. This developed in my own house, carried through school, into motherhood and this is where the rubber hit the road for me - to see how my own daughter felt about the world.

From my first day of school my mind was busy; not with how I felt but feeling the energy of those around me. It was like radio interference, but at five years old how does one verbalise this? I can confirm I didn't. Instead, I just cried and vomited up my corn flakes from that morning, which then required the teacher to call home on my first day. Not an ideal start.

I use the word *'felt'* because, to me, being sensitive is all about how one feels life. It's only when a challenge presented itself in school, for my daughter, that years of self-questioning answered itself.

I found myself reaching out to the teacher for support as my daughter was coming home most days with a pain in her belly and very tearful. First stop was the doctor, but I always felt it was more holistic help she needed. Listening to how she felt about things at school, her interpretations of situations were far too familiar to my own recollections of events. But now I feel I can help guide my own sensitive child with techniques that I know would have helped me so much all those years ago.

Once I had ruled out any physical tummy trouble, I reached out for teacher support and explained that my daughter *'felt things deeply'*, that she was a sensitive soul who loves hard and is loyal to her own detriment. After a trip to Bríd, my ten-year-old daughter began her own journey into self-knowing and understanding; what causes her belly to feel tight or when tears fall from her eyes uncontrollably. On that day, Bríd handed Romy a stone to use as a tool to earth her thoughts, which my daughter named Freckles. Freckles has literally become her rock, her comfort, her support. Taking Freckles to school where her teacher embraced the idea and was keen to understand how and why Freckles had a positive impact on her with no judgement. More and more in the many professional roles we hold, we need to look beyond conventional conditions. Being sensitive in today's world is a true gift.

In our home we have little rituals, grounding techniques, shielding techniques and techniques for cutting the ties, these all form part of our toolbox. The following are some of our rituals:

- On a full moon we will put pen to paper and release any worries that have been building up. On the last full moon, my son affirmed he *"had nothing to release this full moon"*.
- We go to the sea and *'walk away our fears'*, breathing in positivity and out negativity.
- We always take time to *'Ground, Ground, Ground'* bringing us right back to earth.

Avoidance

I was recently chatting with a mum about her sensitive son. She was saying how confident her little one is. He will frequently put up his hand, like a traffic police officer and very firmly say the word NO. The child is three and recently started in crèche. The adults who encounter this behaviour generally laugh at his assertive personality. This behaviour can be displayed when some children come near him to play, or it can happen with extended family members. Meanwhile he is very happy to let other children (previously unknown to him) into his space and plays happily with them. He is not always consistent with who he wants to allow near him.

We talked this through. The little boy is using this method as a safety tool. He has worked out that he doesn't like how he feels in the company of some people. Or there may be someone he usually plays with but occasionally does not want to be near them. Thankfully he is not biting or physically hitting out at others. Instead, he is firmly instructing them to stay out of his space. While this may seem a better option, it is not going to work long term. When he moves into primary school, his demands for his classmates or teacher to step back will not be tolerated. Likewise, his family, and extended family members will have occasion to go through an entire range of emotions as they experience daily life. This tool needs to be traded in. The transition to primary school will be very challenging. Currently people are laughing at and accepting his NO. Within a few months this NO will be reprimanded and have consequences. This child needs new tools.

As he grows and learns about his sensitivity, his gut/intuition will help him discern whose company to avoid and who he can trust. In the following chapters, several suggested tools are described which can be tested to find his best fit. There is no point telling this child to stop saying NO, when in company of those with strong personalities or those experiencing emotional turmoil, without first providing him with an alternative option. His NO is his current coping skill and is stopping him from feeling overwhelmed. Children are not going to give up their favourite toy unless there is something better on offer. Right now, for him NO works.

Grounding

Feeling grounded and connected to our own body is key to knowing which feelings are ours. Grounding helps us to be less impacted by the emotions of others. If someone is sensory and is feeling grounded, they will still pick up on these emotions. But the more grounded they are, the less they will be impacted. Also, the more solid one is in their own energy, the faster they will realise when they *are not themselves*. They will realise

147

the feelings they are experiencing have been absorbed rather than being their own true feelings.

Humanity is very resilient when faced with adversity. At some level, the sensitive person is intuitively aware of the need to feel grounded. They may not comprehend why they need to do a particular exercise, or why they have developed certain habits - but they do know they feel better when doing so. Children, in working this out, implement their own version of grounding. Many come up with ingenious and unique grounding tools but not necessarily healthy ones.

Contact

One young boy realised he felt better when his body made full contact with something solid. The more overwhelmed he was, the more contact he decided he needed. He took to literally running at the wall in his bedroom. When his chest made strong and physical contact, he felt calmer. He would then turn and run at the opposite wall. He would continue to run at the walls for as long as it took him to feel solid. He described it as *'feeling like himself again'.* He had developed this method as his *'go to'.* He knew it worked but didn't know why the contact with something solid helped him feel like himself again.

Even though his habit hurt while making hard and physical contact with a wall, in the absence of any other strategies, this was all he had in his toolbox. When he started school, he would tell himself everything would be ok when he got home. The more overwhelmed he felt, the more he thought about making full contact with his bedroom wall. His family has come to accept this as his coping technique. Long term this is not going to work.

I met a little girl who hit herself in the face with her teddy when overwhelmed. Another child hits their cheek with their hand. The more distressed and difficult their day, the harder and longer they hit themselves. As these children feel the physical pain it reconnects them with their own bodies. All three children have worked out that when they are grounded, they are not overwhelmed. They just need safe grounding practices to replace the damaging, maladaptive ones.

The Wigglers/Movement
Some children use movement as their way to disconnect from others. They develop habits whereby when stressed they keep moving their legs. Others will keep shuffling in their chair as if they were trying to get away from some unseen discomfort. For others it will be their hands or fingers, tapping on the desk, clicking a biro, or touching the tips of certain fingers. Some will

concentrate on blowing air between their teeth, especially if they are missing a tooth. Others will play with or pull their own hair. Their feet may keep moving or perhaps their hips or shoulders are unable to stay still.

This is the tool they have developed to self-regulate when stressed. Telling such a child to *'SIT STILL'* or *'STOP MOVING'* is effectively telling them to stop using the technique they have developed for regulating in difficult circumstances. If an adult gets annoyed with them for their inability to be still; the sensitive child will feel and absorb a copy of this annoyance. This will add to their need to be a wiggler, rather than enabling them to calmly participate in life.

Crying
Practically every sensitive person I have encountered uses crying to let out the pain. After all, that is the purpose of tears. Generally, people crying are doing so because something sad or difficult has happened to them, and they are shedding their sadness or grief. The sensitive child will have their own sadness. They will also have additional sadness because of the lack of understanding from society of their needs. Furthermore, as sadness is such a strong emotion, which everyone experiences frequently; the sensitive

child will often be taking on copies of other people's sadness.

Crying is possibly the healthiest tool children can add to their home-made tool belt. Unfortunately, the more they cry, the more likely they are to be teased by others. Again, adding to their own sadness. Many learn to do their crying on their own. It is not healthy to feel we must hide our emotions. For healthy relationships to develop we need to be able to say to our loved ones how we are feeling. If a child learns not to cry, for fear of reprisal, effectively they are learning not to express their emotions. They carry their sadness until such time as it is safe to cry. Or they learn to shut down.

Water

Some children will have worked out that they feel better when they wash their hands. While shaking off the water they are washing off the copies they have absorbed. Effectively washing off whatever they have sensed was threatening to overwhelm them. Rational thinking can be hard when in a space of fear. Yet the mind can come up with all sorts of imaginative ways to deal with the perceived threat. The problem with this solution is that it will not be possible to access water every time they are in emotional distress. Yes, this tool works, but there needs to be a backup plan. The following story tells of a child who uses water as his solution to combat his fears. Although it is not sensitivity that is driving his anxiety, the example can be applied to all who are overwhelmed and have gone past the point of rational thinking.

JOHN'S JOURNEY
CLAIRE

Our son of seven years of age was afraid he was going to get sick, therefore he started washing his hands constantly throughout the day and using hand sanitiser. His fear of germs grew and he found it very difficult to eat and drink. He stopped playing his favourite sport as contact with people was hard for him to cope with. Eventually, he stopped sitting down as he thought other people's germs were on the chairs, he would stand up all day and not touch anything. His family were not allowed to touch him, or he would have to shower immediately. We admitted him to hospital when it got to the point when he stopped eating and drinking for us.

During these couple of months, we heard about Bríd and the work she did. We made contact with her. She asked us to send on a picture of our son. After a day, we saw a slight change in his demeanour and after a couple of days, he sat down on a seat for the first time in weeks. We kept Bríd informed of his progress and she kept doing her work on him through the picture we sent. Eventually our little boy started to come back to himself. I am truly thankful to Bríd for what she did for our son, it will never be forgotten.

Sound

The use of sound can be very therapeutic. Gentle music, wind chimes, melodies and lullabies can all be aids for helping any distressed child feel calmer. One empathic person, I was recently speaking with, explained how she uses sad songs as a trigger to connect with her emotions. Having been teased throughout her childhood for crying she has learnt to lock away sadness - both her own painful events and those she absorbs from others. When she is on her own, she plays songs with sad lyrics, she then cries out all her sadness. She literally pulls the plug on her bathtub of stored tears and allows them to flow unabated, until every drop has been shed. Exhausted but relieved she can participate in the world again, storing up all painful emotion until she again feels the need to play her music and safely pull the plug.

Some children will shout or scream, use whatever implements are available to bang, or pound their feet, as if in a temper. Each is endeavouring to release the emotional pain that is overwhelming them.

These are the tools they have adapted for their personal use. Using loud noises, they are endeavouring to rid themselves of the emotional turmoil they are inexplicably experiencing. They are trying to get the attention of others. For those with limited speech, noise may be the only way they can highlight their plight. Unfortunately, these tools can work against them. Their apparent outbursts may not be received well by others, resulting in negative consequence or reprimands.

The annoyance experienced by the caregiver will also be available to the sensitive child. Having tried to empty out their emotional bathtub of tears or scream out their distress, they are already soaking up the new emotional annoyance and disapproval of those witnessing their attempts to release all the pain previously collected.

Additionally, many of these children will frequently be in fight or flight mode, due to the unpredictability of their emotional lives. For those using screaming or noise as their release, the noise they are creating is, at the same time, hurting their ears. You may have witnessed children screaming while covering their ears with their hands. As discussed previously, our hearing changes when in extreme anxiety, prioritising loud and low sound. The tool they have developed as their '*go to*' is adding to their distress.

A MOTHER'S LOVE
GRACE

As a mother, who is an empath herself, I still have mixed emotions about having an empathic child. I know, in my heart, it is one of the most beautiful gifts in the world. In that it can give you a real appreciation for the beauty of nature and the value of others, and ultimately can be of service to others. There are days where the '*mother worries*' can outweigh the beautiful gift. I know for me; I just want to protect him from the world forever. Even though I know in my heart of hearts, he will have to make his own way. I have known that my son is an empath since he was born, I just knew. He was the type of baby that would observe and watch everything. He would also cry when his older sister would cry – which was a small clue. As a young toddler now, I often wonder how I can help him protect and nurture himself and that is where Bríd comes in.

Over the last few months, I have had a very erratic toddler. He has just been quite angry and tearful. One moment he could come up and give you a hug, smile brightly at you with a gorgeous smile and melt your heart. A minute later he could take something and throw it, hit his sibling, and scream and scream until all the distress and annoyance is out of his system. Knowing my son, I could tell he was stuck in a cycle that was not ending. One day, I thought of Bríd, and wondered to myself if she could help? I was struggling with his behaviour and how to handle it, so I decided to reach out. I sent her a picture of my son and Bríd kindly agreed to do the healing for him.

When she phoned me back, she mentioned that my son was in a hyper-vigilant state. He was watching to see how everybody was doing and taking in a copy of their feelings. She really helped me with tips and strategies to sooth him. She reminded me to talk to him when the tantrums have passed; reminding him that he is safe and that he is loved. She also helped me with some grounding strategies for him – things like running on the grass barefoot, jumping up and down, being close to the ground on his belly. She suggested some additional tools for when he gets a bit older, like imagining he is putting all his anger/worry etc. into a stone.

When Bríd completed her healing, my son came home that day and screamed and screamed. It was as if he was getting everything out of his system. I stayed nearby, to make sure he was safe, and I just allowed him to get it all out. Once that was done, there was such an improvement in the way he was around the house. My happy-go-lucky little toddler was back again and I could just tell something had shifted and changed for him. It can be hard to quantify in writing at times, but a mother knows, and I know that whatever was distressing him had moved out. I am beyond grateful to Bríd for using her gorgeous and magical gifts to help my son and I am so grateful for her support. As a mother I just want the best for my son, and I want to be able to support him on his journey.

I am fully aware that those whose approach to life is more academically based may not be open to my work as a Spiritual Healer. But I ask that this not cloud the mind-set of the reader on the topic of sensitivity. My spiritual beliefs are in no way intended to influence the reader, it is for each of us to come to our own understanding and relationship with our concept of a higher power. Whether you believe in the presence of a creator, or not, I would ask that you remain open to the fact that people experience differing levels of sensitivity. This topic needs to be discussed and understood.

In my work I use my sensitivity to assist me in identifying any physical or emotional pain my clients may be experiencing. With my personal belief, I believe in the presence of a God, a creator who is loving and supportive. My beliefs have been influenced both by the family I was born into and by my own personal experiences. Having identified the client's individual blocks and issues, I ask for Divine and angelic intervention. With this little boy I prayed that he would be disconnected from all energy/emotions other than his own and that he be returned solid in his own body, energy, and emotions. One does not need a healer to pray on behalf of another. If you believe in a higher power, who is loving and supportive, then why not ask their assistance to alleviate the distress of a struggling child? While those with different beliefs, can be empowered with the knowledge of various grounding tools, explained in the following chapters.

Humour

When faced with heavy energy the sensitive child may choose to lighten the atmosphere through humour. They will use wit and jokes to bring others to a good mood. They themselves may not be feeling light-hearted but this may be their coping mechanism. As those in their company start to laugh and raise their vibration, this higher energy is then available to the empath to soak up copies. If this is their only coping mechanism, there may be times when their humour or seeming indifference is not received well. Others may perceive their humour as disrespectful and inappropriate.

If in their past they have been teased for being sensitive or for crying, they may choose to be the comedian rather than the target. It may be less painful to joke at their own expense, rather than be teased and ridiculed by others. As they get older, they may give up trying to please the adults. Instead, they become the class clown deciding to make themselves the centre of attention for their social group's approval. They have decided to get other children's notice and friendship by appearing not to take life seriously. But all the while they crave approval and a way to make their life easier.

CHILD FRIENDLY
EXPLANATIONS

When I am speaking with young children about their sensitivity, I need to explain their challenges and abilities in a child friendly language. This gives the child a vocabulary to explain their struggles. For most adults, it is hard to grasp the true meaning of sensitivity, with all its complexities, challenges, and versatilities. How much harder therefore, is it for a young child to comprehend sensitivity? *"Someone who is aware of other people's needs, problems, feelings or pain and shows compassion for what the other person is going through".* Reading this definition to a five-year-old is not going to help. Firstly, the adult needs to have an in-depth understanding and then find child friendly wording.

Radios

The main explanation I give children is the comparison to a radio. I ask the young child to think of their heart as a radio. If everyone's heart is like a radio; each heart is playing its own station. The person presses a button to hear what is happening on someone else's station. They then become aware of that person's feelings. The owner of the radio decides what station to listen to. It can be playing happy, or it can be playing sad, maybe it's playing angry or jealous. Then life happens and our feelings change. Everyone has their own radio. Everyone has their own station. As we go about our day, we continue to receive information from other people on their stations. We decide what station to listen to. We are in charge.

However, for sensitive and empathic children their personal station can be interrupted from day to day, even from minute to minute, without having pressed any buttons. Their radio is different to that of most people. It can pick up on other stations. But for them, the other stations are coming in on top of their own station without warning. The additional information is being received while the child is trying to listen to their own station. This causes problems for their radio. They may turn off the radio (switch off) or risk having multiple stations playing at the same time (sensory overload). It becomes very difficult to concentrate, to decide how to respond, or even to participate.

When a child understands what is going on, they start to make sense of their reactions. They can start to work out, in daily settings, which is their station and

161

which stations are not theirs. Generally, they can also identify who the other stations belong to:

"The sad station is mummy's".
"The angry station belongs to Johnny".
"The scared station belongs to Rose".

Once they have a vocabulary, and adults to share this conversation with, their world changes. With this invaluable piece of their jigsaw, they are ready to learn coping tools. They can start to discard the old unsuitable tools and begin to accumulate specific skills that they can use in their daily life. They now understand why they need the tools. Now they can learn how to keep their radio serviced and the importance of keeping it in good working order (grounding). Separately they learn what to do if their radio does go off station or picks up multiple stations (disconnect).

I ask them to imagine their right thumb is the control button for their radio. To turn off other stations, I get them to take their left hand and encircle their right thumb. With light pressure, they imagine, they are twisting the button and turning off all the other stations so that they are back listening only to their own station.

Once a child can use the control button, we can now discuss its use in more detail. Whether they still need to switch off, or do they now feel safe to be present in their bodies? They learn to function from a place which is true to their own feelings (or from their own station). I explain how clever they were to come up with their own coping techniques, but that it is now safe to let them go. To get the radio to work they no longer need to engage in such activities as hitting themselves, running at a wall, screaming to block out noise, body wiggling - until other stations stop playing. If in reality we owned a radio which was not working, we may be tempted to shout at it, hit it and get frustrated with it but this is not going to fix it. Having turned off all the other stations it is now safe to be present. We can now encourage them to breath into their lungs. While they do so, we can add the mantras *"It is safe for me to be here"*. To then breath into their feet until they feel stuck to the floor *"It is safe for me to be in my body"*.

When the child is older, it will be possible to teach them further about the emotional information they are picking up on and how to appropriately help those in emotional turmoil. For the young child, however, what they need to learn is which emotion is theirs. They can then be aware of the other stations, who they belong to, and how to interact appropriately. There will be days when they are still overwhelmed, but they will be able to turn off all the other stations.

One morning a mum had made an appointment with me for her five-year-old son. When they parked outside, I could hear the little boy crying. *"No Mammy, please Mammy, I can't go in".* This little boy is extremely sensitive. Trying to coax him to get out of the car and go into school had become a daily challenge. Prior to attending school, he was a happy little lad, he loved interacting with his family and playing with his toys. His two previous years were during the Covid outbreak, with enforced lockdown restrictions. His interaction with others was at an absolute minimum. Since starting school, he was constantly distressed and cried frequently. On speaking with the teachers, they could offer no explanation, as they were not aware of anyone treating him badly.

The mum finally managed to persuade the little boy to leave the car and come inside my home. He did as she requested but was quietly crying as he stood behind her. This child is empathic. He is accustomed to life at home with his family and feels safe there. Once he started school he was constantly overwhelmed by the energy of others. He was relaxed entering his own home and visiting relatives. He had become accustomed to their personalities. But he was now terrified of having to enter any other building. This extended to shops, church and even play centres.

With the reassurance of his mum, he entered my hallway but was simply unable to come any further. He could not step inside the treatment room. I sat a chair in the hall for him and put a chair inside the door for his mum. I sat in the opposite corner to him. He could see me but was at a safe distance, so as not to be afraid of my presence.

While he sat there, I explained to him about his very special heart. I explained that his heart worked differently to most people. I gave my example of the radio. That his heart was like a radio picking up different stations at the same time. I told him how brave he had been every time he had gone to school, and how brave he was coming into my home as his radio was trying so hard to work. This was the reason life has been so difficult for him since he had started school. But after today it didn't need to be that hard anymore.

After that talk, the child's demeanour visible changed. He sat straighter in the chair. He made eye contact with me. He then came into the room without being asked and stood in front of me. He asked questions - as he started to make sense of his life and realised it could be easier. His questions then took a different direction, as he asked if he could pick up on the stations of animals. He said he always knew how they felt. His next question was about his hamster. Could people with special hearts pick up on the station of a hamster? He said his hamster was tired, but was happy when he came home from school, and played with her. Realising this was a special ability, that most people do not possess, he grew in confidence. A little earlier he had cried and pleaded with his mum not to come into my home, let alone walk without persuasion into my treatment room. Now he had come into the room without encouragement and was happily chatting and asking questions. He knows he is now in charge of his radio.

Once children come to an understanding of their special ability their world changes dramatically for the better. With this knowledge they can then start to collect suitable tools. I explain that people need to take care of their radios. It needs to be kept safe and not get damaged. As with the radios, we need to take care of ourselves and keep ourselves in good condition. Our radio will then work better and pick up less stations. When it does pick up a different station, we will notice straight away that something is wrong. In addition to being able to turn off the radio stations, we need to practice being solid. Grounding and self-care are important for everyone but for the young sensitives it is essential. I have included a chapter on this subject ('*Grounding*') with numerous suggestions that can become part of everyday life. The more solid the child is in their own energy, the less they will be overwhelmed when their radio picks up interference.

Sweaters

Children in heightened anxiety or who are continuously switching off, may not be able to remain present long enough to hear and comprehend the radio example. They need a quicker explanation, but one interesting enough to hold their attention. If you have the care of a child whose concentration drifts, I suggest you ask the following question.

"If your sweater/tee-shirt had a feeling-name today, what would it be? Its feeling-name is the same as your feeling".

The child then names their sweater, Happy, Sad, Tired or whatever they are feeling at the time. Naming others in their family or friends, ask the child to name those peoples sweaters.

"Timmy?"	*"Funny"*
"Aunty Mary?"	*"Busy"*
"Uncle Tom?"	*"Angry"*
"Baby Joey?"	*"Happy"*
"Miss Smith?"	*"Cross"*

The conversation then continues. *"Some people with special hearts collect an invisible copy of other people's sweaters. These sweaters don't fit properly, as they don't belong to you. When we put on an invisible sweater it changes how we feel. Even though you can't see the sweater, you will know you have one on. If you put on little Timmy's sweater, you would be saying and doing silly thing. Aunty Mary's sweater would have you running around in circles, all day, and getting nothing finished. With Uncle Tom's sweater your tummy would probably be upset, and you might be mean to your friends. Baby Joey's sweater would have you giggling all day and with Miss Smith's sweater, you wouldn't have any patience and not listen to what others had to say. How many invisible sweaters are you wearing today? But don't worry, I know how you can take all these invisible sweaters off, as they don't belong to you. Then the only sweater you are wearing, is the one with your feelings. We will work this out together".*

Computer Programme

I ask the child to imagine their brain as a room with lots of computers. The computers have different tasks. Some tell the body how to work and when to move. Others help with school and all the new things we have to learn. Some store our memories. One computer tells us how to think and what to think. And one computer is for our feelings. It tells us if we are happy or sad, tired, angry, jealous or in pain. I call this the '*Feelings Computer*'. It helps us work out what we like and dislike, where we feel safe and who we love.

Sometimes the Feelings Computer can take a photocopy of someone else's feelings and enters this new copy into the sensitive child's computer. Their mind is now running two emotional programmes simultaneously. The stronger the emotion they have copied, the more likely it is to override their own programme. This can have differing results. They may assume the new programme and behave accordingly. Alternatively, they may switch in and out between the two programmes.

Simple wording
For younger children these examples may still be too difficult to comprehend. The wording needs to be shorter with definite direction.
"You seem very sad/angry. Will we blow the sad/angry out the window?"

GROUNDING

Once children have an understanding that being sensitive simply means they are sensing their environment; they can then start to collect appropriate tools and let go of the ones that don't work. Their toolbox will need two separate sets. The first set of tools will help them remain grounded. The second set of tools will be for when they feel overwhelmed by the energy of others.

Picture two children. One is wearing canvas sports shoes. The second child is wearing wellingtons (gum boots). Both children step into a big muddy puddle and start to play. The canvas shoes start to soak up the muddy water. The more porous the shoes, the more they allow the mud to soak in. They continue to absorb the mud until they are completely saturated. At this point, the child in the canvas shoes can no longer play because of their discomfort.

Wellingtons are made of rubber. Like the children from my story on farm life initiation, whoever is wearing the wellingtons is grounded, and has the appropriate footwear. If they step into the mud - nothing will be absorbed. The boots may get a bit muddy, but the child can play for as long as they desire. They can continue to participate in the game. The more sensitive someone is, the more they need to be like the child wearing the wellingtons. The greater their level of sensitivity; the greater their need to be grounded. To achieve this, specific types of activities are required to form part of their daily lives.

Life can be busy, especially in homes with young children, where there are continuous demands on the adults' time. It will not be possible to fit in all these activities daily. Nor is that what I am suggesting. As the child learns which tools suit them best, they will start to pick their own tools. Exercises like playing a football match or swimming may only happen occasionally. Whereas two minutes jogging on the spot, jumping jacks/star fish or skipping can be done intermittingly throughout the day. Like all exercises, the time needed to practice grounding exercises will vary as well, depending on the child.

Imagine every time the child participates in a grounding activity, they are filling their *'grounding tank'*. Major activities give the child a *'grounding reserve'*. This reserve will be of huge benefit when faced with a situation that is highly emotionally charged. The more they have in their reserve, the more they will be able to cope with their sensitivity challenges. It will also help them remain calm enough to realise when their radio is picking up a different frequency.

Grounding activities can be divided into different categories:

- **Nature**
- **Impact**
- **Concentration**
- **Logic**
- **Sound**

Nature

Not surprisingly, time spent in nature will help with grounding. Connecting with our natural environment whether this is countryside, seaside, garden, park or even trees planted along the footpaths. Spending time in nature helps children to ground and be present.

- **Walks**: Ideally at a pace where they can observe their surroundings and bring their breathing and mind into line with nature. By observing nature, their attention switches to the pace of the elements. A warm day heats and relaxes the body, while a windy day can blow away the cobwebs. Frost (or Jack Frost) brings magical ice patterns in ponds and puddles and rain can wash away the troubles of the day.

172

- **Gardening:** Depending on where the child lives, it may be possible to be involved in gardening. Working with the soil has a strong positive effect on the child's temperament. Planting flowers or vegetables, weeding or tending to the garden are all grounding activities. As they fill their watering can and go from plant to plant, they are connecting with the earth.
- **Cooking/baking:** Like gardening; measuring ingredients, working the dough, breaking up butter, whipping an egg, washing, and preparing vegetables, all these tasks can help to ground, through contact with natural produce.

Impact

We read earlier about the boy running at the wall. He believed he would feel better as he felt the impact of the wall against his body. The impact was helping him to feel more connected to his own body, and less overwhelmed even though, at times, he was hurting himself from the force of the contact. Thankfully there are easier and safer ways of doing this.

- **Physical activity:** When we think of impact, we possibly first think of physical activity. Games which involve running and jumping, all help us to feel connected to the earth therefore, feeling more centred in our own energy. When we run and jump our feet are meeting the earth with force. The greater the impact, the more we feel the connection.

- **Dancing:** All types of dance movement help us feel grounded. Whether jazz, tap, jive, ballet, or traditional dance movement; the more force placed by the foot the more beneficial the action.

- **Sitting on the floor:** When a child sits on the floor/garden/pavement with their legs stretched out in front (as opposed to sitting on a chair, mat, or cushion) they are connecting with the ground. By encouraging the child to play on the floor, or perhaps occasionally sit on the floor while reading, the contact with the ground will help them feel more solid. Likewise lying or crawling on their tummy will have the same effect.

- **Being barefoot:** Walking barefoot outdoors, if location and climate allow, is very calming. Otherwise, some time spent without shoes, while indoors, is beneficial.

Concentration

- **Movement combined with focus:** Gymnastics, dance, climbing or skipping all add an extra level of grounding. In addition to impact, these activities involve concentration. The child needs to be focused on the task in hand. Otherwise, they will trip, fall, or get the routine wrong. Their

174

thoughts are solely on the task; therefore, they are completely present in the moment. During dance class, concentration on the new steps is required and while doing this the entire focus is on the dance move.

- **Sports and group activities:** In addition to running, or whatever the activity involves, the child must concentrate on the rules; their position, the position of their teammates and the position of their opponents.

- **Art:** While working out what to draw, which colours to use, concentrating on colouring inside the lines, the amount of pressure to apply, the child must focus and thus be present.

- **Crafts**: Again, concentration is required while following a pattern, using scissors, doing needle work, beading or pottery, etc.

- **Music**: Learning a musical instrument, whether by ear or reading sheet music involves focus. Alternatively, if the child likes to sing, whether attending singing classes or learning songs from the radio, they are focusing on the words and airs.

Animals

Animals, especially dogs, have been man's best friend since humanity first started to develop emotional bonds. Whether farm animals or house pets all require care, bedding, food, water, and exercise. When a sensitive child is tasked with their care, the animal becomes the focus. There are many benefits to spending time with pets. Some pet farms '*lend*' out their rabbits to children who have certain emotional or physical diagnosis. The parents comment on the calming effect of this generous gesture.

- **Pets:** When children are fortunate enough to have pets, they gain from the contact with the animal. They will not feel judged by their pets, whereas they can feel judged by humans. Many children confide in these animals, telling them about their day, their struggles, sadness, and joy. Pets can become '*unpaid counsellors*' irrespective of the secrets shared, they will not criticise, condemn or make fun of their owners. They demonstrate the characteristics that are vital in a counselling session: non-judgemental and unconditional positive regard. If having a pet is not feasible perhaps it's possible to volunteer with the care and exercise of animals at local animal shelters.

- **Horse riding:** Children who participate in horse riding learn to observe the movement and mood of the animal. They need to divide their attention between the animal's response and the obstacles in their surroundings. To be successful they must work as a team. For many sensitive

176

children who participate in this activity, the rhythm of the movement also adds a layer of comfort, their body adjusts to the rhythm.

- **Dog walking:** For dog owners, walking their pet is a daily task and becomes routine. Generally, when introducing new activities, it is easy to skip a day: the weather doesn't suit, tiredness, lack of motivation, more interesting pastimes or distractions may present. Forming a habit, through regular repetition, can be challenging. When there is no choice but to carry out an activity – the habit is formed. While dog walking, there is a responsibility to focus on and connect with nature.

One note of warning regarding pets; some people will be impacted, on a sensory level, by the energy of their pet. In the chapter on *'Child Friendly Explanations'*, I introduced a little boy who was picking up on his hamster's station. When this happens, the child will need to be encouraged to switch off the animal's station and disconnect. This is the topic for the next chapter.

Logic

- **Numbers and puzzles:** To calculate the answer or participate in the game, to any level of competency, one must bring their focus solely to the task. This can be maths equations, card games, puzzles, crosswords, etc. Setting a simple maths challenge can help the child feel grounded and less anxious. *"What class are you in now? And what age will you be when you finish school?"* To give the correct answer, they must use logic.

SUGGESTED MATHS GAMES

- During car/bus journeys, children can play a game observing number plates of other vehicles. Each participant picks a number sequence for example 211, 212 or 232. They count how many times they see the sequence before they reach their destination. To do this they will have to read every number plate they pass, bringing their focus to the numbers.

- Alternatively, all participants on the journey, pick a specific model of car. Every time they see that car make; they get a point. Whoever has the most points by the time they reach their destination wins the game.

- There can be a game involving road signage. In turn, as each sign is passed, those playing the game say what the sign was and what it means.

- Count how many different county registration plates they pass during the drive. Or participants are each allocated a county to identify.

- I spy. This game is probably the best known for trying to pass time while on a long journey. One person leads '*I spy with my little eye something beginning with the letter c*'. The others observe their surroundings and guess until one identifies the correct object beginning with that letter (e.g., car, cottage, church). The person with the correct guess goes next '*I spy with my little eye something beginning with the letter w*'. The other participants guess until this object is identified (e.g., wheel, water, window) and so on until participants lose interest.

- Count all the green doors they pass.
- Count all the green cars they pass.

While walking with children the above games can be modified to suit the child's interests and abilities. Any of these games, or similar activities, help ground the participants and helps their concentration.

Numbers and puzzles are tools which help the child to feel more solid in themselves. While calculating the answer they are not thinking about anyone else, they are more likely to be solid in their own energy. These games are also very beneficial to those who tend to be in fight or flight mode, as it shifts their concentration away from their fears and anxieties.

NUMBERS ARE MY FRIENDS

Numbers are my friends. That may seem like a strange sentence but throughout school and my earlier careers, calculating figures meant I had to concentrate and focus solely on the task. Even in primary when I could not recite tables no matter how long I spent learning them at night. I worked out a way around this problem. If I could not remember the answer to 4×7, I broke it down to a sum I could do. I knew $7 + 7 = 14$. I would then add $14 + 14$ to get my answer.

When I finished secondary school, I did a secretarial course. The opposite of what a dyslexic teenager should be doing; considering the typewriters at the time were manual and did not have a spell-check facility. On finishing secretarial school, I headed to London. My first week there, I got a job as a secretary with a stock broking firm. Coming from a rural background, I was ill equipped for this new life (also I hadn't mentioned in the interview my struggles with spelling!). However, a few days into my new job, the accountant was having difficulty balancing a spreadsheet. I offered to have a look at it for him. In good humour, but expecting no great results, he gave me the books. I quickly found where he had failed to carry over an entry.

Following this incident, he went and spoke with the owner of the company. On his return, he informed me I would no longer be working as a secretary. Instead, I was to move onto the stock broking floor. I was now a 'Settlements Supervisor'. I had absolutely no idea what this job involved but knew it meant numbers and calculations, rather than letters and spellings. I loved my new job. Despite being surrounded by brokers in constant anxiety, flickering between moments of exhilaration and moments of deep disappointment, I remained grounded and unaffected by their emotional roller-coaster. Every career I have held since my stock broking days, has had a financial element. I think of numbers as my friends.

Before we start to encourage a child to participate in grounding activities, they need to work out what activities bring them joy. This may seem like a ridiculous statement. Children who are sensitive are aware of the emotions of others. They feel the annoyance of others and they also feel when someone is happy. These feelings are absorbed, often overwriting their own programme. The child believes them to be their own. So, it is in their personal interest that those around them are happy. Thus, they tend to develop as the people-pleaser discussed in the chapter, *'The People-Pleaser'*.

Sensitive children often speak and think as *'we'* rather than *'I'*.

- *"What game will we play?"*
- *"Where will we go?"*
- *"What will we do?"*
- *"Who will go first?"*
- *"Who will I be in the game?"*
- *"What position would you like me to play?"*

Is it easier to allow them to continue as people-pleasers? Where they never say *'no'* and follow the group consensus or the stronger personality. Is it easier if they are not solid in their own desires? Yes, it may be easier in the short term to let them please others and not feel strong enough to know/express their own needs. Long term, this is not healthy and does not bode well for their futures.

The more grounded they are, the more they develop their unique individuality. The more they will express their opinion. They learn how to appropriately say yes or no. This will help them, as they grow, to make better decisions in their friendships and their important life decisions. They will gradually learn to form personal boundaries.

The more solid they are, the more they will discover which grounding tools suit them. They may enjoy ballet or prefer to be part of a rugby scrum. Maybe their talent is baking or a specific type of craft. As they learn to be an individual, they will discover their own skills and hobbies, they will learn what brings them joy. The activities and hobbies which bring them joy are their keys to living a more fulfilled life. It is their key to being able to participate in social settings, and emotionally charged environments.

Spending time doing grounding activities which suit their individual needs, will build up a reserve. It is as if they are charging their battery. With their battery charged, they are ready for school and activities in social settings. During school breaks they can recharge their battery. Some classroom activities will also help them recharge; be this reading, maths, art, or crafts. The more they are aware of what fulfils them, the more they will feel the benefit of the exercise.

DISCONNECTING

Once the sensitive child understands why they can feel so overwhelmed without warning, they will then need two separate sets of tools going forward. As mentioned, the first set is their grounding tools. These are essential for every child. These self-care exercises not only aid with grounding, but also increase ability to cope and to regulate when they encounter life challenges. By identifying and spending time doing what they love, they are developing a greater understanding of self and individuality.

The second set of tools is specifically for the sensitive child. This is for the times they have taken on a copy of the feelings of others. It is for when their radio station is picking up interference from one, or perhaps, multiple stations simultaneously.

Ultimately, whichever disconnection option the child settles on, they are forming a mind-set. When they perform this action, it will effectively restore their radio to their own station, removing the overlaying stations which overwhelm them. Different tools will suit different children, depending on their age and what feels appropriate. The choice of tools is endless. The challenge is to find the best option(s) for the child. Similar to a construction worker with numerous options in a hardware store, the child will choose the tool(s) they feel most appropriate for themselves.

After we are born, we learn to tell the difference between light and dark. We know if we are hungry, in pain, in need of changing. We start to differentiate sounds, to identify 'our' people. Since then, everything else that we have learnt has been programmed. Our vocabulary, how to eat, which cutlery to use, how to sit, to socialise, the rules of every game, what behaviour is expected. Every action has been taught or copied. Our beliefs are all formed by observing others and from information available. We have been trained. The sensitive child now needs to be trained to perform a certain action to disconnect from the energy of others. This action is accompanied with the intention/belief that they are effectively, stepping out of the feelings of others, and returning solid in their own energy.

SUGGESTED TOOLS FOR DISCONNECTING
- **Radio**
- **Affirmations**
- **Wash hands/sanitise**
- **Rub it off**

- **Store it**
- **Religious belief**
- **Breath**

Radio

Previously, I gave the example of the child's heart being like a radio. If they are comfortable accepting this as a way of understanding their distress, then this is probably the easiest option for disconnecting. They can imagine their heart as a radio, they then imagine their right thumb as the button that controls the stations. Once aware they are not feeling *'right'* or *'not themselves'* they take their left hand and encircle their thumb. With light pressure, they imagine they are twisting the knob and turning off the other stations so that they are back listening to only their own station.

Affirmations:

In the meditations *'Being Present'* and *'Coming off the Cliff'*, I included sentences reassuring the child that they are sufficient and are accepted.

- *"I like who I am".*
- *"I am learning more about myself every day".*
- *"I am learning how to be calm".*
- *"I am learning how to be still".*
- *"Right now, I am safe".*
- *"I know I am good enough".*
- *"I am in control of my own mind".*

Affirmations can also be used for disconnecting. They can be used on their own, or the sentence can accompany the chosen action. Thus, strengthening the new belief.

- *"I am now my own person".*
- *"I'm taking off all the sweaters that belong to others".*
- *"I am strong in myself, strong in my own energy".*
- *"I am solid in my own energy".*
- *"I disconnect".*
- *"I am completely myself".*
- *"I am me".*
- *"Switching off their station, switching on my station".*
- *"I step out of the puddle".*

Whatever sentence makes the child feel strong and completely themselves, will be most effective. Once the child understands why they are doing this, they start to let go of their fears. This in turn reduces their anxiety and the amount of time spent switched off, or in fight or flight mode.

Wash hands/sanitise.
We all wash our hands repeatedly throughout the day, even more so since our introduction to the word 'Covid'. Hand washing on its own is not going to make any

changes to the sensitive child who is in overload. There must be a new computer programme set. The concept is that when overwhelmed, the child can wash off everything energetic they have collected, which is separate to their own true feelings. Ideally use cold water. As it runs over the hands, the cold water helps bring an awareness back to the body. The programme being set is *"I am washing it away"*. *"I'm washing off all energy except my own"*. *"Washing it down the plug hole"*.

Alternatively, they could splash cold water on their face, though this could present other problems. A young child could use this as an excuse to splash water and create a mess in the bathroom, or the school washroom. In our current era of sanitising (to lessen the spread of virus) the programme could be set every time the child uses hand sanitiser; they are cleaning off energetic copies, as well as protection from the virus.

Having a bath or shower is not going to be possible in a school setting. When at home showering/bath-time can become a *'spring clean'* exercise. If the child has had a particularly challenging day, they can imagine they are thoroughly washing away absolutely every bit of energy. However, we don't want to create a panic situation where this must be done or else they won't feel better. We don't want the child to think they have to scrub their skin or that they must get every bit of their body soaped down thus creating a fear. *"What will happen if I miss a bit?"* *"What if I don't do it right?"* *"What if I don't wash it all off?"* It needs to be introduced in a reassuring and calm way. *"As I lie back and relax it will **all** float away".* *"While I relax and close my eyes it will **all** wash down the plug hole".*

Rub it off.

The child is being encouraged to *'rub it off'*. They wipe their thigh with their hands. Pressure is applied on the base of their hands while contacting their thigh. Alternatively, they can rub their right hand along their arm from the shoulder to the elbow as if they are dusting it off. Mentally they are reassuring themselves *"I am wiping it all off, I am completely myself".*

Store it.

The child is encouraged to imagine taking all the excess emotional trauma they have soaked up and put it into something to be released later. This can be their pencil case, or their pocket. When they get home, they can unzip their pencil case or turn their pocket out, letting go all the excess emotional pain. Perhaps a second pencil case can be provided for this specific purpose.

Often children find a new concept easier if there is something they can see or touch. In my treatment room I keep a box with small '*magic*' stones. The stones contain quartz. For children old enough to understand the concept, I explain how quartz is used in computers and mobile phones to store data. I explain this stone will never run out of storage capacity. The child holds the stone in their left hand and imagines all the pain and sadness they have accumulated leaving their heart and travel down their arm into their stone.

With younger children I simply tell them that these are magic stones and they can put all their sadness into them. I ask these little children to hold a stone of their choice in their left hand and '*feel*' all the sadness leaving their heart and travel down into the stone. Being sensory, the children love how the stone feels and just holding it can bring comfort. Previously, we were introduced to Romy by her mother and learnt how she has named her stone Freckles. We read that **"Freckles has literally become her rock, her comfort, her support"**. Like Freckles, the stone can be given a name and become their special tool for disconnecting.

It may not be appropriate, or wise, for a child to carry a stone around with them! I suggest that if their parent/guardian is driving/walking them to school the stone stays in the car or the adult ensures its safe keeping. The child holds the stone before going into school, to help them feel calm and let go of anything they have already taken on prior to the school gate. On leaving the school, their stone is on standby to receive the troubles of the day.

Depending on their belief system, they can put the stone on the windowsill at night for the fairies or angels to take away all the pain. If their parent/guardian feels it's appropriate, they can add a little request to the fairies or angels to take care of whoever owns the distress. Another option, following a particularly emotionally challenging day, is to wash the stone on returning home and imagine all the distress being washed down the plug hole.

Now we meet Romy who is the owner of Freckles.

FEELING THINGS
ROMY O'NEILL
(AGE TEN)

I walk my dog in a field at the back of my house and one day I went with my brother and my dog Penny on a walk. We saw a dead rabbit and I burst out crying. I instantly felt a pain in my heart. I thought, this is just an innocent rabbit and I felt so sad for it. I ran home to my Dad, explaining we needed to go back and bury the rabbit, so it was safe from the foxes who lived in the field too.

Dad thought something had happened to my brother because I was so upset when I ran home to explain why I needed help. We went back to bury the rabbit, but he was gone. Dad and I had a torch to see if we could find it, we searched for a long time - we never did find him. I know it's nature, but it still makes me so sad that the rabbit died and was just left there alone.

The rabbit is one example of how I feel about things. After a while of getting tummy aches, my mum who likes energy things, brought me to meet Bríd. I felt she really understood things I said and helped me make sense of everything. My tummy aches were because of things I was thinking in my head or feeling from those around me, maybe from the schoolyard or activities. I was sometimes feeling things that belonged to those around me.

Bríd helped me develop a little toolbox for when my head would be fizzy with thoughts. Like the thoughts about the rabbit. I now swim in the sea and have a rock called Freckles that keeps me grounded when I feel fizzy in my head.

Religious belief

This suggestion will depend completely on the belief system of the child and their family. If appropriate, the child could be encouraged to pray along the lines *"Please God/Source help whoever owns the energy (or the sad/tired/angry feelings) that I have picked up on today. I ask to be disconnected from all feelings other than my own. I ask to return completely to my own feelings. Thank you"*.

Breath

Everyone will be familiar with the suggestion that we could breathe deeply to reduce stress in difficult circumstances. The breath can also be incorporated as a child's ritual for disconnecting. They are encouraged to take a deep breath whenever they feel their senses overloaded. Then, they imagine blowing away everything they have picked up, on a sensory level, out of their body. This can be taught as a single deep breath or maybe three deep breaths.

- **Red Dots:** In the earlier chapter *'Coming off the Cliff'* I described the Red Dot breathing exercise. Red dots are placed in key locations throughout the building. On seeing the dots, all children are taught to breathe deeply, in through their nose, and out through their mouth. The red dots can be placed randomly at home, or at school, and the children are encouraged to take some slow deep breaths whenever they see one of the red dots.

- **Me, myself, and I:** The child takes three deep breaths in through the nose, and out through the mouth. As they take the first breath, they feel the breath entering their body, and out loud or quietly (whichever is appropriate) the say the word ME. They take the second breath, and again feel the breath entering their body, and now say the word MYSELF. As the third breath enters the body, they say the word I. In this way they are re-connecting with their own bodies. While using the breath and the words Me, Myself, and I they are disconnecting from the feelings of others.

- **Bubbles:** Weather and time permitting, playing with bubbles can help younger children disconnect. To play they must breathe deeply and fill their lungs to blow the bubbles through the plastic wand and send them floating into the sky. In addition to the deep breathing their concentration is on the bubbles, where they go and how high they float. They are completely enthralled with the game.

- **Fairy Breath:** One breath exercise I teach children is what I call the '*Fairy Breath*'. The child takes a deep breath in through their nose. They then blow out slowly through the mouth. Unlike normal breathing, they barely part their lips in the centre so there is only a tiny passageway for the breath to pass through. Then, they blow gently out through this tiny passage, with the imagined gentleness of a fairy's breath. The air takes longer to blow out. By the time there is absolutely no air left in their lungs, they have returned strong and calm in their own power. This exercise will not draw any unwanted attention to themselves.

These disconnection tools are meant to make the life of the child easier, and not draw attention to them. During class if they start to feel their radio picking up different frequencies, and then believe they must take three deep breaths, and blow them out forcefully - other children will notice and may not understand. This could possibly lead to teasing. Whatever the chosen tool, it must be easy and discreet for the child to use.

As the child comes to terms with their special abilities, age-appropriate conversations can start to take place. If they have accepted the radio or the sweaters or the overwritten computer as their concept for understanding their sensory overload, then this will be the main starting point of the conversations.

- *"How are you feeling today?"*
- *"How did school feel today?"*
- *"Did you pick up on different radio stations/sweaters/computer programmes today?"*
- *"Do you know who the radio station/sweater/computer programme belongs to?"*
- *"Let's wash it off/wipe it off."*
- *(If appropriate)* *"Will we ask God/Source to take care of whoever owns the sad/anger/pain?"*

Once disconnected from the energy of others, practicing a short and easy grounding exercise would be very beneficial. Again, this may need to be discreet, as we do not want to draw the attention of others. This can be done out loud, or the child can be taught to do it silently in their mind. In a previous chapter, *'Switching Off'*, I introduced an exercise which I teach to assist switching back on. When we notice the child functioning from a place of limited emotional capacity, I suggest that once they have been reassured and feel safe to do so, they can switch back on. As the first breath fills their lungs, they can tell themselves that *"it is safe to be present"*. With the second breath, they imagine the breath going all the way down to their feet, as they do so they tell themselves that *"it is safe to be in my body"*.

196

- **Brain teasers:** Maths sums are another very quick way to do this. Depending on the child's age, after changing radio stations, or taking off additional sweaters, they can be encouraged to do their times tables. Perhaps the adult could just pick two random sums for the child to answer.

  $7 + 3 = ?$

  $8 + 2 = ?$

Or

  $12 \times 8 = ?$

  $7 \times 9 = ?$

- **Tongue twisters:** These also force us to concentrate (and bring in a light heartedness).

  Red leather, yellow leather – repeated three times.

  Unique New York – repeated three times

  She sells seashells by the seashore but the shells that she sells are seashore shells, I'm sure.

  Betty bought a bit of butter, but the bit of butter Betty bought was bitter, so Betty bought another bit of butter to make the bit of bitter butter Betty bought better.

- **Spelling:** A challenging word can also be a quick and easy way to ground. Depending on the child's age and ability that can range from CAT to MISSISSIPPI.

The child is now armed with an understanding, in child friendly terms, as to why they get overwhelmed. They have grounding skills to use daily, which fill their grounding reserve tank. The more grounded the child is, the less they will be impacted by the energy of others. They will still be sensitive to their environment, but it won't overwhelm them. Healthy tools have been provided. These can be tried and tested, to assess which ones match their individual needs and abilities. Simple grounding skills are on hand, to help them regulate once disconnected.

With their tool belt complete they can let go of their old tools e.g.: switching off, screaming, biting, scrubbing their skin, harmful physical contact, and withdrawing from the world. They are equipped to form an integral part of their society.

IMAGINATION

Imagination is a wonderful ability. It allows us to invent and to be creative. New concepts are formed and solutions found. For some, imagination can become a safe place for escapism. Being switched off is different to using imagination or daydreaming. When one is switched off, they are functioning without being present emotionally. No new concepts or thoughts are being formed. The person is simply going through the motions. Time has lapsed, without thought, other than for the task that is required. For many, not just those who are sensitive, imagination can be a way of coping with difficult situations. It is a wonderful healthy ability, but not somewhere to go for hours daily. It is not a safe crutch to adopt for coping with challenging times.

Imagination is part of childhood. Making up games, playing doctors, or shopkeepers, helps the child understand their environment. This interaction with their dolls and teddies, helps them work through their day. Occasionally, their toys are the only safe friends for a child to confide in.

For many sensitive children imagination/day dreaming is the tool they adopt for coping with emotional overload. Once they understand why they feel different to others and have new tools, their need for imagination lessens. We don't want to stop a child from being creative. Perhaps they can be encouraged to write stories, plays, poetry, songs or put on a puppet show. The amount of time spent in *'imagination land'* can be monitored, like the amount of time spent on gaming or electronic devices. The child using imagination has literally gone away to their magic land. We need to be careful when asking them to return to this reality. Raising our voice can startle or shock the child. Whispering or lowering our voice, while making direct eye contact, may have a calmer affect.

Their imagination can be harnessed and encouraged in a productive way. A special notebook provided for drawing their creations, designs or stories will help the child feel more positive about themselves. Instead of indefinite periods spent in escapism, time can be allotted, resulting in achievements through creativity. Once the child has returned from imagination land to reality, some form of grounding exercise would be beneficial. This would be helpful for all children whose imagination has removed them from reality. For the sensitive child this is essential. They have returned from a place of creativity and happiness and with their hearts completely open and joyful. Unless they ground themselves after their escape, their heightened level of openness and sensitivity completely exposes them to their surroundings.

In the earlier chapter on grounding techniques suggestions included music, song, and dance. When one is learning a new piece of music, song lyrics or a dance routine; they are completely focused on the task at hand. As they become proficient, the level of concentration lessens. For many who are musical, once they are confident with the piece, they can immerse themselves completely in the emotion it evokes. You may be familiar with the term '*the voice of an angel*' used to describe certain singers. For the listener it seems some performers are '*other worldly*'. For these singers and performers, they are completely immersed in the emotion. When they have finished their recital or repertoire, some simple breathing exercise will help them return solidly into their surroundings.

Artists of all ages can also immerse themselves in their creations. They have stepped from logical brain to abstract brain. Once they have finished their creation, or take a temporary pause from their creative task, a few moments grounding would be advisable.

Our ancient ancestors lived in constant danger. Life was extremely precarious, hence the need for the body to develop the fight or flight process. Yet despite the constant threat of danger, and the struggle for survival - they took the time to draw. Prehistoric drawings and carvings have been found throughout the world. Images of animals form the majority of these ancient art pieces.

Many of the drawings show the primitive man being victorious in the battle over their prey. These people took the time to create a structure to stand on, to enable them to reach the ceiling of their cave simply to draw. Did these drawings serve another purpose? If we look at an image of ourselves in a position of strength every day, it increases our confidence and self-belief. For the caveman, waking up and going to sleep looking at a drawing of himself killing a bear helped him feel empowered. Logically the bear is bigger and stronger than our ancestor, who is armed merely with a stick with a sharp stone perched precariously at the end. Yet we know these people had a high level of success - as they survived. Evidence from archaeological digs indicate the use of fur for clothing and animal bones used as everyday utensils.

Simply taking the time to imagine their success did not create the desired outcome. The bear didn't suddenly surrender on realising there was an image of him being killed carved on the ceiling of the cave. Drawing an image of our desired outcome and bringing it to our awareness increases our confidence. It also focuses our thoughts on what we do want from life and ways to achieve that result.

The bear may not have surrendered, but the hunter had less fear. He approached the bear in a calmer state of mind, allowing himself to focus on what needed to be done. Where to stand, to wait quietly for the right moment to strike. When anxious, it is difficult to make logical decisions. The cave man believed he would be victorious and his thoughts helped this to become a reality.

FOOTBALL

One day I observed children playing football. One child had his head down. As he walked past me to participate, as instructed by the coach, I heard him say *"What's the point? No one will pass me the ball anyway"*. And this was very much his reality. The entire time he was on the pitch, he had his head down. He didn't make eye contact with any of his teammates, didn't call for the ball and didn't tackle any of the opposition. He truly believed he would be excluded by the others. Even when the ball came close to him, he didn't see it as his head was down. His thoughts became his reality.

Another child, smaller in stature, ran past me onto the pitch. As he ran, he was telling his friend *"I'm going to score"*. This child chased every opportunity to get the ball. He made himself available and called to his team mates to pass to him. In turn he passed the ball to them. And yes, he scored. His thoughts became his reality.

Imagination can be used as a powerful way to focus children. Manifesting has become a buzz word in recent years for inviting in universal abundance. When used properly it has many advantages. Drawing and colouring help with grounding. First, we must think what to draw, what would we like the outcome to be, how do we imagine that outcome would look? We identify what are our priorities in life and what changes we would like to see happen?

A word of caution with encouraging children to manifest - it must be realistic. If their Aunty is terminally ill in a hospice, then drawing her back home making pies is not going to change the outcome. For children from low-income families, drawing a new home with expensive furnishings is not in itself going to create this.

Where addiction or abuse are prevalent in the child's environment drawing a picture and possibly adding words *"daddy is nice to everyone" "mammy is always sober"* is not going to work. When introducing children to manifesting, it needs to be explained properly.

When children are asked to imagine and draw what their future adult home will look like, this is healthy. It encourages the thought process that they can be successful to get this lovely house. To achieve this outcome, they consider how they can be the orchestrator of their destiny. They will have to put effort into study or find the right job. They may draw a future partner and children in the picture, setting the belief that they are loveable and can one day be surrounded by people who love them. By drawing their upcoming football match result, they are increasing their confidence and self-belief, which in turn, increases their chances of victory. *"I'm going to score"*.

For the sensitive child, creating images of themselves fully participating in the classroom, without being overwhelmed, would be a place to start. It would increase their confidence and self-belief. Perhaps they could draw themselves smiling while wearing a virtual sensitivity tool-belt, complete with magic stone, bubbles, football shoes, tennis ball and a dog lead. Believing they can embrace their sensitivity, understand it and manage it, they could draw themselves enjoying different busy, social settings. Words can be added to the picture to strengthen their conviction.

- *"I love being me".*
- *"I love that I have a sensitive heart".*
- *"I feel safe in the classroom".*
- *"Today is a good day".*
- *"I can turn off the feelings of others".*
- *"I am in charge of my radio station".*

Their thoughts are focusing on what they really want and they realise it can become their reality.

Perhaps the entire class could focus on an outcome they would like to see happen. Again, this needs to be realistic. If working on '*world peace*' this will not occur in one day. However, the manifesting through drawing and wording helps the child focus on the desire for peace. This is what they want the future to look like. They are setting the belief that countries will accept differences, and offer support, instead of hostility. If every child was to set this belief their future would be different. We can all create, we can all manifest, we can all learn to think positively about ourselves.

ADDITIONAL CHALLENGES

Earlier I gave the example of the child's heart like that of a radio, in which they pick up on the stations of others. Some children with extreme sensitivity can also tune into other environmental stations. Each child will have differing levels of sensitivity. Different senses will be more acute than others with their awareness drawn to different energy vibrations.

Some will be frequently upset, feeling sad and overwhelmed without being able to explain why. Some will pick up on events that happened in a room prior to entering it, or just feel uncomfortable in certain settings. Even though to the standard eye, it is simply an empty room.

Earlier we read the story 'Socks' submitted by Florence: "For me as an empath, it feels natural to merge with my children at some level as a way of *'being with them'*. At times this gives me valuable insight. However, I now recognise that this can get in the way of letting my children develop fully into their own selves, in their own right. Also, if I in effect, *'join them'*, then I lose the chance of being genuinely clear and available to them, and it can lead to issues being magnified rather than calmly addressed. I am now better able to maintain my energetic independence from them as needed. Essentially, I am more myself for more of the time, which allows them to be more themselves more of the time."

There are many stories of identical twins being aware of how the other was feeling, or if they were in difficulty, even when in separate locations. Highly sensitive people will also be impacted by the feelings of their loved ones, even when in different locations. This can make it harder to identify who is in emotional distress. My own sister lives in Australia. When she was ready to give birth to her daughters, I knew she was in labour without being told, as I was also feeling contractions. We are connected energetically to those we have a strong bond with.

Thunderstorms, heavy rainfall and even changes in the moon will impact people differently. Others will sense the presence of souls. Some will be aware of future events, without any logical explanation. Each child is unique, and so it is with sensitive children. There is no one definition that fits all. The level at which people are affected, by these different types of energy, will depend on their personal level of sensitivity. The greater the level of sensitivity, the greater the impact of the environment.

Residual Energy:

The sensitive person knows how someone is feeling without being told. They sense the feelings of others and take on a copy of those feelings. Many can also sense their environment. When they walk into a building or an empty room, they may feel a sudden heaviness or uneasiness, but for no apparent reason. There is a change in how they feel, but the explanation is not apparent. The room simply does not feel nice. When a traumatic event has occurred, the memory of the emotions experienced previously are held within the environment. Some will feel these emotions on entering the space. Likewise, objects such as furniture, jewellery, books, artwork, tools and even clothing can hold these memories. For those who do not have the ability to sense residual energy this may seem far outside the realms of possibility. But for some this can be part of everyday life.

Geopathic Energy

The earth has its own magnetic energy field, which differs to other planets. All life forms have developed over time to living within this magnetic field. The brain sends continuous signals to the body enabling us to function. However, there can be interferences in the magnetic field. For example, if there is a narrow stream of water below ground, this can create its own electromagnetic field. It can distort the natural resonance in that area. If a property is built over certain mineral concentrations, fault lines or underground caves systems, they can have an impact on the vibration in that area. Some believe man-made constructions, for example underground railways, electric pylons and masts can adversely affect those who are highly sensitive.

Déjà Vu

Déjà vu is the common term given to describe when one feels they have already witnessed or experienced an event, prior to its occurrence. It can include believing you have heard something, or have been told information, prior to receiving the knowledge.

Out of Body Experiences:

An out-of-body experience is a phenomenon in which a person perceives the world from a location outside their physical body. The most common stories on this experience are those of people who survived comas, or after their hearts stopped, and they were medically pronounced dead. These people have described scenes they witnessed, while their bodies were not functioning. Many sensitive people believe they have out of body experiences while asleep. For others, they may have had this happen while in a deep meditative state. On waking they are aware of information, which is not available in a logical way, perhaps an accident, a conversation they have '*witnessed*' or information on the health/wellbeing of a family member.

Angels

The word angel is defined as: *"A spiritual being believed to act as a messenger of God."* Conventionally, angels are represented in human form with wings and a long robe. For those who have this belief system they may, on occasion, sense the presence of an angel. Others will describe visions where they have seen or communicated with angels.

Soul Energy

Many highly sensitive people believe they are aware of the presence of Soul Energy. Whether you (the reader) believe this to be real or not, such an experience for a child who believes it to be real, is very frightening. Yes, this may turn out to be a figment of an active imagination or role play, as they come to an understanding of the concept. However, some children have experiences, following which, they can describe the name, appearance, and personality of someone deceased when they have no other way of coming to this information.

Each of these subjects are vast topics, with numerous books and information available. Everyone is unique and will have unique experiences, and so it is with the sensitive child. The adult is unlikely to be able to answer every question, on every topic, on which a child may require information. If a child is describing something, which seems outside the experience of the adult, but for them seems very real, some reassurance and research will be of great comfort. For a child to know they can trust an adult and share their thoughts and experiences (both real and imaginary) is an invaluable gift.

The following story was sent in by the mum of a sensitive little girl. We read how the mother endeavours to support and empower her daughter, while protecting her from the expectations and perceptions of others. A challenge for any mum.

NAVIGATION
CATHY WHELAN

I knew Mae was special from the moment she was born, even more so when she started talking at ten months and singing at fourteen months. It was like she was here before. She has the biggest heart and the kindest soul, but we now know that comes with an array of challenges.

As a toddler it was obvious, she was more sensitive than others, she had an incredible sense of how others were feeling. In the beginning it was subtle, like giving hugs to those who really needed them, unbeknownst to the fact. This later progressed to getting upset during story time. For example, the story of 'The Ugly Duckling' made Mae burst into tears when the duckling's family left without him, it was as if she could feel his pain. Sensitivity to films and the News soon followed. When Mae was four, we were on the way to the playground one day when she started sobbing uncontrollably. Now, like most, I was only half listening to the radio whereas the little lady in the back clung to every word. It had been reported that a young boy had died in a road traffic collision. Through the sobs she asked me what collision meant and from that day on, I also paid attention to every single word. The radio is now immediately changed at the hint of bad news. I must admit that this aspect of parenting a sensitive child is challenging. How do we navigate exposing her to the world around her, while protecting her at the same time?

Mae was a daydreamer from a very young age. So much so, I was convinced that there was something wrong. Did she have ADD, or autism perhaps? Being a teacher myself, my mind was on overdrive. I discussed this with my Mam, who very quickly reassured me that Mae was perfect and just had a very good imagination. That was an understatement!

At the age of three, Mae had multiple bowls set up on the kitchen table for her imaginary friends. She would be in full conversation with them. I told myself that it must have been an only child thing as Mae didn't have a sibling at that point. At three and a half she told us that there was a man in her room, to which my husband searched the house in a blind panic. Thinking back still makes me smile. When we asked her what the man said to her, she told us that he said, *"Go back to bed, good girleen"*, so she did. We agreed that it must have been her great grand-uncle John as we had recently renovated his house and had just moved in. In the beginning we presumed we were sleeping in John's room, the largest room upstairs, but in later years we discovered that Mae actually sleeps in his room which all added up. It fills me with happiness to think that John was checking in on her and I also like to think it was John's way of giving us his seal of approval. We now have a picture of him in our hallway, alongside Mae's great grandparents who have passed, and we sing him Happy Birthday every year. I think it's so important that my children know who he is and how grateful we are to live in his beautiful farmhouse.

Since the man in her room scenario, Mae has kept her daydreaming adventures to herself. At times, it has been challenging to bring her back into the room when she is on another planet. Abruptly calling "*Mae!*" upsets her as she thinks she's in trouble. One evening while eating dinner, myself and my husband unintentionally called her name in unison to get her attention. She began to cry and through the tears told us that she didn't know how he was going to get home. When we asked who, she said *"the man on the bike"*. She went on to tell us that he was here to see his friend and that his bike was broken. I suggested that I could give him a lift home, but she told me I couldn't because he was a stranger to me. When I insisted that I didn't mind because she knew him, she was annoyed and didn't want to talk about it anymore. It was at this point that we realised Mae would never have told us about this man, only for the fact that we shocked her into it and secondly, Mae was aware that I didn't know him but couldn't quite articulate why. From that moment on, she no longer wanted to discuss it. I attempted to bring it up at a later stage to which she told me, *"That was just my imagination Mammy"*. As her parent, I worry that she carries a lot on her shoulders in silence. How many souls has she encountered? Have they all been kind? And just how much has she been exposed to at such a young age?

Mae has asked about the *"people in the sky"* since she could talk. It fascinated her from an early age, and she has asked every question imaginable at this point. Initially, I put it down to being a bright firstborn, but we quickly discovered that Mae was much more than that. She longed to know everything about her great grandparents who had passed on and used to get upset that she never met them. I'll never forget the night she asked me if I missed them, her bright eyes brimming with tears, and I had to be honest and tell her that I had no memories of them as they had all passed away by the time I was two and a half. Her next question was *"But does it make you sad that you missed them Mammy?"* and quite frankly yes, it really does. It is baffling when your five-year-old is the one asking the big questions and making you reflect on your life. When I see the love between Mae and her grandparents, I really wish I was given the same chance.

Speaking of grandparents, Mae was very fortunate to have had two great-grannies up to recently. She always worried about when they would go up to the sky and asked this question a million times. In her little mind she decided that they would reach one hundred and then go up, but she didn't like to think about this for too long. Thinking about her granny and grandad missing their mammies made her very sad. On the flip side, we explained to Mae that when the time came her great-grannies would be reunited with their husbands, who they hadn't seen in nearly twenty years! We encouraged her to think about this instead, and to imagine how happy her great-grannies will be when they see their husbands again. When her great-granny did pass away earlier this year, at the amazing age of ninety-seven, Mae had us all smiling through tears by telling us that Great Granny Cathy was definitely going on a date with Great Grandad James right about now!

As time passed and Mae began to ask the bigger questions, we had to explain to her that people can pass away at any age and that it's not just older people. This conversation was drip fed over a period of time as Mae's little mind immediately raced to, *"But you won't die until you're old though Mammy?"* It is so difficult to explain reality, while also trying to protect her sensitive soul and, in my experience, when I ask other parents' advice they are generally bemused as their children have never even broached the subject!

Mae is now seven and has completed her first two years of school. Her teacher describes her as *"quietly confident"*, which really sums her up. At her parent-teacher meeting, I was told that Mae always checks on the children that are upset or feeling left out. I beamed with pride during that meeting. It really is a superpower to be kind. On the flip side however, Mae can burst into tears in the car because her friend at school was sad. She seems to struggle to detach herself from the feelings of others which makes life all that more difficult for her. All in all, she has had a wonderful first two years of school and long may it continue. I would advise any parent of a sensitive child to meet with their teacher and explain how sensitive they are. Even by explaining that Mae gets upset when her name is called abruptly certainly avoided some upset. Also, by explaining that it is not in Mae's nature to make up stories, I felt the teacher understood that if Mae confides in her, it is something that is genuinely upsetting her. As a teacher myself, I would greatly appreciate the forewarning.

Mae's world changed dramatically before her fourth birthday. The arrival of a cute baby boy made her a very proud big sister. Life was wonderful during the baby stage and then he grew up! Mae's little brother absolutely idolises her, but boy does he give her a hard time! From eighteen months onwards, this very determined individual put his stamp on everything. Anything Mae had, he wanted. Any drawings she did, he destroyed if he got his hands on them, and anything she built, he broke. She put down a tough twelve months of this carnage. To be honest, I don't know how they have the same genetics! They are the definition of polar opposites. Now that he's nearing three, things have significantly improved. Some reasoning on his part and some strict parenting on ours has certainly helped. They have an indescribable love for each other and are the best of friends for about two hours a day!

At times, the struggle of parenting through this stage got me down. How did we get it so right with the first and so wrong with the second? Bríd was such a help with this internal conflict. She explained how Mae's little brother was sent here for a reason and despite the fact that they are so different, he will be (and already is) her biggest protector. On reflection, I can see that now. In his near three years of existence, he has taught Mae to stand her ground, to say no, to fight back and, to truly forgive. I try to remind myself of this in the midst of World War III!

Bríd was wonderful with Mae. She openly spoke about the people who can't get home and very kindly offered to help these people for her. All Mae has to do is let me know and I'll text Bríd. This has opened a much-needed communication pathway between us. Bríd also broached the topic of Mae taking on the feelings of others. She described it as putting on other peoples' jumpers, a sadness jumper, an anger jumper, etc. Mae could then see how her own jumper was being hidden by others.

Bríd gave her some useful coping strategies to help. She showed her how to acknowledge the feelings of others and then to wipe them away or blow them out the window. I do hope that Mae uses these strategies whenever she needs them. Bríd also advised Mae to walk away from her little brother when he is upsetting her and to tell him that she isn't playing with him when he is not being nice. This has definitely helped. Jack craves her attention and approval so much, that walking away is the only thing that really makes him reflect on his behaviour. These strategies have greatly helped us all.

I am so grateful that I had the pleasure of meeting Bríd and that I can turn to her for advice on how to navigate the future. Perhaps Mae will shut herself off from her *"imagination land"* or perhaps this will be something that we will need to guide her through, who knows? All I do know for sure is that if she does turn it off, she will come back to it at a later date and when I am gone, my very special little lady will be aware whenever I check in on her. How lovely is that thought?

A sincere thank you to you Bríd for your guidance, and I am truly grateful to Mae for choosing me to be her mammy.

THE ANCHOR

A child's level of sensitivity will be greatly influenced by their parents' levels of sensitivity and emotional capacity. If you, as an adult, are on the upper side of the builder's spirit level of sensitivity - you too will need to acquire an understanding of this ability and acquire your own grounding and disconnecting tools. As a sensitive individual you too may be a people-pleaser without a strong sense of self, and without healthy boundaries. Much of what you have read in previous chapters will have resonated, and hopefully helped you put some of your jigsaw pieces together. Perhaps you have come to a better understanding of your own childhood. To help children in your care come to an acceptance of their abilities and learn to incorporate their skills into their daily lives, you will need to lead by example. Your own challenges may include:

- Coming to a better understanding of sensitivity, empathy, sensory overload and recognising those with narcissistic tendencies.
- Accepting you are of equal value to your peers.

- Learning to speak as an I, instead of always WE or YOU.
- Implementing personal boundaries without guilt.
- Working out your own grounding skills, some that you enjoy and can fit into your schedule without seeing them as chores.
- Learning to self-care without guilt.
- Paying more attention to your senses.
- Being aware of your own feelings.
- Identifying which tools you are already carrying in your tool belt, for occasions when you feel overwhelmed.
- Observing if you are switching off as part of your everyday life and practice taking breaths and switching back on.
- Observing if you are anxious and/or in fight or flight mode. If so, observe the thoughts that are driving your anxiety and replace with sentences that are positive, honest, and reassuring.
- Accepting that being sensitive is not a weakness.
- Accepting yourself.

Adults who are highly sensitive/empathic must first come to an understanding of their own emotional capacity before they can truly assist others. Should you

find yourself saying statements like those listed below -
then take note of what you are trying to bring to your
own awareness.

- *"I'm not myself today"*.
- *"I can't understand my reaction"*.
- *"That's just not like me"*.

Self-care can be very low on the list of priorities for
those who have the care of any child. Let alone a child
who is struggling to find their place in society, to find a
place where they are accepted. So many adults spend
their days waiting for help and expert advice. As they
wait their own needs are also left waiting.

WAITING
M.R.D.

As I wait here the night before my children start back
at school, my mind fleets back to all the times we as
mothers are waiting...

Waiting for the birth, 1 week overdue.
Waiting for the first cry and waiting to check his
toes and fingers.
Waiting for his first solid spoonful.
Waiting for his first crawl, first step.

Waiting for his first word.

The waiting list goes on. And here I am with an eight-year-old and a ten-year-old and the waiting still goes on. Additional needs are a whole different waiting game. Now I'm waiting to get resources, to get help and to be heard. Waiting for experts to tell me my next move, my next goal, my next step.

"Waiting" might sound innocuous but in my world, it causes immense anxiety, worry, fear and anger. As I wait for my autistic son to take his place for the first time in a *'special school'.* I wait on the side-lines in awe of how he manages to cope in a world not designed for him. I'll wait for him to arrive home, off the school bus, for the very first time… anxiety eating into every cell of my body.

"Did anyone play with him?"
"Did he understand anything the teacher said?"
"Did they understand his attempts to communicate?"
"Did he miss me; our snuggles, our kisses, our songs?"

I wait to know all this… But I may never find out the answers… Living in the world of non-verbal autism makes us wait infinitely for answers. So, I may never know the answers. The only thing I do know is that he is protected from afar. An angel resides over him. An angel I loved with every fibre of my being. His namesake.

"Lord, help me to accept the waiting I must do, help me not to lose heart and help our family unit to keep strong for each other."

Anchors

Previously I gave the comparison of collecting copies of sweaters that belong to others as we go about our daily lives. Imagine a sensitive parent picks up a duplicate copy of a colleague's/ customer's sweater and does not disconnect. That parent is likely to bring a copy of this new invisible sweater home. Everyone who lives with this parent, who is also sensitive, will take a copy of the new invisible clothing. If mum is highly sensitive and has a colleague who suffers from depression, she will be taking on a copy of her colleague's emotion every time she meets that colleague. When the workday is over and mum returns home to her sensitive offspring, she will be bringing home more than groceries. These children have not met the person suffering from depression but are aware of the new energy from their mum. The mother and the child/children may now find themselves lethargic, lacking motivation, and without joy.

When the sensitive child attends school, sports, or organised events they are open to collect invisible sweaters - belonging to their friends or teachers. Bringing the new clothing home, they then pass a copy to their sensitive sibling/parent. When we have more than one highly sensitive/empathic person living together, we can experience what I refer to as the *'Domino Effect'*.

When two sensitive people come together emotions can escalate out of proportion to the event that is triggering these feelings. Have you ever had an argument with someone where, for no apparent reason, it got blown out of all proportion? This could also be the domino effect.

Take a scenario where a mother, Sarah, and her daughter, Kate, are both extremely sensitive. Kate is nine and has just mastered showering, washing her hair, drying, and dressing herself. She is quite proud of this achievement. She has just showered using the correct amount of shower gel, shampoo and conditioner, has thoroughly rinsed her hair, has dried, and dressed herself. She notices the bathroom plants are very dry and in much need of water. She goes to the kitchen and gets the watering jug. Having watered the bathroom plants, she then decides to do the same for all the household plants.

Her mum walks past the bathroom and sees damp towels on the floor with dirty laundry beside them. She calls Kate to come to the bathroom. Sarah is annoyed and starts criticising Kate for not putting the towels and clothes in the laundry. Kate is upset, she had been so proud of her achievements and fully intended on tidying up afterwards. She had become distracted with a chore she felt would make her mother happy. Kate tries to explain. Her mum is getting annoyed. Kate, now in defensive mode, is raising her voice. Mum is now raising her voice and getting angry. The situation has escalated out of all proportion.

Mum is in a copy of her daughter's energy and her daughter is in a copy of her mum's energy. While Sarah was having her shower, mum was already feeling exhausted and stressed after a long day. On finding the damp towels and laundry she felt disappointed and annoyed.

Kate had felt proud of her achievement and with the fact she had watered the neglected plants for her mum, she was not expecting criticism. Her sweater now reads *"victimised, sad and misunderstood."* Mother and daughter now start the process of taking on copies of each other's sweaters.

Mum = exhausted + disappointed + annoyed.
Kate = victimised + sad + misunderstood.

Now they add a copy of the other person's feelings on top of theirs.
Mum = exhausted + disappointed + annoyed + *victimised + sad + misunderstood.*
Kate = victimised + sad + misunderstood **+ exhausted + disappointed + annoyed.**

Now they take on a copy of each other's new energy and the situation starts to escalate:
Mum = (exhausted + disappointed + annoyed + *victimised + sad + misunderstood.)* × 2
Kate = (victimised + sad + misunderstood **+ exhausted + disappointed + annoyed.)** × 2

Their emotions continue to escalate exponentially:
Mum = (exhausted + disappointed + annoyed + *victimised + sad + misunderstood)* × 3
Kate = (victimised + sad + misunderstood **+ exhausted + disappointed + annoyed.)** × 3

Instead of the evening being a proud moment for mother and daughter, as Katie moves a step towards independence and adulthood, both are distressed and disappointed. When the adult reaches an understanding of their hyper-sensitivity, they can then explain it to

229

their children. This will help prevent future situations getting out of hand and improve family relationships.

Many parents of sensitive children had to work out ways to cope in a society, in which their own sensitivity was not embraced. Healthy options have to be developed by these adults, for their own grounding and disconnecting from the energies of others. Before they can help empower their children, they have to learn how to help themselves.

FINDING BALANCE
MARIA

I had to try and navigate a very toxic family/school life and felt very unsafe through most of it... I felt it like the whole world was hot and loud and I had to find a place that was cool and quiet... I spent as much time as possible in the local library or getting lost in books when I was at home... I also sucked my thumb till I was about twelve... Interestingly, most of my siblings did too... We were all trying to find ways of shutting out the '*real*' world as it was too overwhelming. I'm now a people-pleaser and constantly vigilant as to who is going to shout at me, if I'm in a very unfamiliar environment. One unmentioned result of this sensitivity is that I was way too sensitive to the needs of my children, to their detriment. There were times when my over protectiveness was not of help to them. It's very hard to get the balance right.

Real life happens and it is impossible for an adult to be in a good mood twenty-four seven. By ensuring time for self-care, adding in grounding practices and bringing an awareness to the times when they *are not themselves*, parents will be offering a steady anchor to children in their care. When they are not in good form, there is a logical explanation for the change in their humour, which the children can understand. They will know what to expect. On days when the child is wearing the invisible sweaters of others, their significant adults will be in a steady, reliable emotional space to assist them disconnect and ground themselves. They will be able to offer the child an anchor to steady their vessel.

Kelly, a primary school teacher, has kindly shared her observations on the many challenges young students are faced with - many of these concepts barely within their comprehension. We see how she encourages the children in her care to tap into their feelings and identify their fears. She then empowers them with tools enabling them to take control.

TAKING CONTROL
KELLY

The following are my observations following S.P.H.E (Social, Personal, Health Education) lessons in a Primary School classroom of nine and ten-year-old boys and girls.

The modern child has a lot to deal with, climate change, the pandemic, the War between Russia and Ukraine, technology, apps, being unfriended, re-friended, obesity levels in our country, image defining people, earlier signs of puberty, gender change, gender confusion, changing families, the blended family, custody, poverty, homelessness, the cost of living, entitlement, bullying, the list seems endless.

These are aspects of life that the modern ten-year-old is aware of. A lot of these aspects of life have always existed but it is the rate at which these phenomena are occurring that is causing the child, of only a decade, to feel bombarded long before their brains have developed enough to process it. They need OUR help, as in ADULT help to deal with how they feel and how they cope. But how well is the modern adult coping with all of this?

From my observations of parents, I am one myself, we may see the world as harsh or hostile. We may try to metaphorically sweep the way clear for our children, keeping the path free of anything that might cause upset. We try to have the play dates lined up, their favourite take-away ready at the press of a button. *"Holiday cancelled? Let us just book a bigger better one. How about tickets to that concert? Would more screen time make things better?"* Yes, we are trying to keep their lives wonderfully charmed and happy and this is a good thing. But are we simply over protecting them and not fully preparing them for our modern world? Do they have the skills they need for that all-important resilience?

I have a poster in my classroom - *"Resilience - to be strong in the face of a challenge"*. It incorporates an image of a superhero character, chest out and head held high. I am quite sure at the start of the year that they don't know what it means but by the end I would hope that most of them do. In the classroom setting we actively discuss our fears, I learn from them, they learn from me. I always try to tell the children that they have a degree of control. Yes, the climate is in crisis but what measures can we do in school to help this situation. Plant the wildflowers for the bees, encourage single use plastics, separate our waste, recycle our batteries and all the other initiatives that our children take part in. It stops it all being so scary when we can do something about it right?

When Putin advanced on Ukraine on the 24th of February 2022, the children were quite shocked at the mention of World War. One child said to me that she thought World Wars were part of history. We watch the news on RTE junior every day and we watched the war play out (the filtered version for children). We eventually came face to face with it when children from the Ukraine arrived into our very classroom. Again, instead of being afraid of this or having fears, we had control. We could not stop Putin, but we could welcome these children into our lives, learn some of the Ukraine language, play basketball or chess, and help them feel part of a community.

One day I asked the children to write down their biggest fear. I collected their answers. Almost every child wrote death, their parents, or their own death, some children even wrote, cancer. We did agree that we have less control over this, but we do have some - keeping our bodies fit, eating the right foods, following guidelines regarding the Covid virus, staying safe in the water and on our roads. It wasn't all doom and gloom.

So yes, our fears are lessened by our degree of control but what if we don't know what our fears are, we can't identify them we just feel bad, anxious, low, or sad. We identify these in the Primary School as the NO FEELINGS. We have NO FEELINGS that we just can't shake that follow us like a *'Black Cloud'*. How can we control this when we don't know what it is? This is where our greater understanding of FEELINGS and our STRATEGIES come into play. Feelings come and go. You can have hundreds, maybe thousands all in the one day. The *'feel good'* ones, the *'feel bad'* ones are all NORMAL. To feel good all the time is NOT NORMAL but equally to feel bad all the time is NOT NORMAL.

I asked the children *"Are our thoughts fears? Are they making us afraid? If so, how do we deal with them? How do we gain control? What can I do?"* We decide that bad thoughts move faster than good thoughts. We drew an image, a character to show what this bad thought might look like, skinny speedy with a nasty smile. One child drew him on paper, and we cut him out. We stuck him into a blank outline of a human head on the white board. Then we discussed how we would deal with him. Children talked about banging sliotars off walls or going for a run, watching a movie to forget about him. Yes, all this can work for a while, but he is still there. I gradually explained to the children that trying to get it out of the brain was only giving it strength. It was resisting, fighting back and its muscles were getting stronger. We were also playing into its hands. It wanted more attention and power and we were giving it by trying to push it out. So, we talked about the strategy of piling good thoughts into our brain and squishing him. I had golden arrows pointing to that head outline and shooting in and filling up the head until he was covered up. We are in control.

Reading this testimonial, my primary school experiences seem like something from the dark ages. Yet compared to previous generations, they may consider my age group as privileged.

A BYGONE ERA

At the primary I attended boys and girls were both taught together for the first three years. We were discouraged from interacting and were teased if we did so. Apparently, once children reached the age of eight, it was no longer appropriate for children of opposite sex to share the same classrooms and play area. The boys left to attend the monastery and the girls continued at the convent.

In first class, (aged six/seven) each boy was assigned a seat beside a girl, but we were not supposed to interact. One day my pencil needed sharpening and I couldn't find my sharpener. I whispered to the boy beside me to borrow his. Unfortunately, our nun saw me. She teased me in front of all my pears. *"Bríd is talking to her boyfriend"*. The other children gave the encouraged response, and all laughed (some nervously). The nun then walked behind my seat and banged my head off the little boy's head. I felt so bad. Not just at being teased, the pain, the injustice of not being able to speak and request a pencil sharpener, but mostly I felt responsible for the pain inflicted on this little boy.

I am very grateful to Kelly for sharing her thoughts and observations. I smiled as I read her sentences on 'NO FEELINGS'. "Our fears are lessened by our degree of control but what if we don't know what our fears are, we can't identify them. We just feel bad, anxious, low, or sad. We identify these in the Primary School as the NO FEELINGS. We have NO FEELINGS that we just can't shake that follow us like a 'Black Cloud'. How can we control this when we don't know what it is?

What she refers to as the 'NO FEELINGS' sums up how I felt for much of my life. There was often a black cloud, but it had no logical reason to be there. I was sensing someone else's black cloud. It is wonderful that some primary schools are having these difficult conversations with their young students. Giving them a safe space to discuss very heavy topics, and reassurance that they can voice their concerns. Hopefully one day these conversations will include how being highly sensitive can lead to these 'NO FEELINGS' and supply the necessary grounding and disconnecting tools.

It is wonderful to know that children now live in an era where they are accepted as individuals and encouraged to participate appropriately in the classroom and in conversation. Schools now include topics that would never have been considered in the past. By segregating girls from boys, they were putting us at a social disadvantage, where we were unaccustomed and uncomfortable interacting with the opposite sex. To see topics on gender, actively and openly, discussed is so progressive. Considering some fifty years ago I was punished for speaking to a boy. It gives me great hope that one day the topic of sensitivity will also be included on the curriculum. Perhaps the day has come when adults begin to understand the mystery of the sensitive child.

By having these conversations openly, in front of all the class, each child will benefit. The obvious gain being for those on the sensitive side of the builder's spirit level. Those who find themselves in the bubble in the centre, will gain a better understanding of their sensitive classmates. Children who are on the lower side of the spirit level, with little emotional capacity, may discover ways to safely engage with their hearts. To open and acknowledging the feelings, including the pain held there, and making room for experiences of love and joy, often so sadly lacking.

THE OWL

The owl has long been the subject of myth and lore, with many confused perceptions, as it is unlike '*normal*' birds. It has great vision and hearing. It can adjust in an instant from a telescopic to a microscopic focus. The pupils respond in a fraction of a second to very minute changes in light intensity. The owl's eyes are specially adapted to detect subtle movements. They have extra light-sensitive cones and rods in the retina to help with this. Even in the darkest of nights, its acute eyesight enables it to pinpoint the exact location of its prey. Its hearing is just as powerful. The ears are asymmetrical, and one ear is usually larger than the other.

In North America the owl was believed to have great healing powers and was associated with mystery and magic. Although other cultures feared it as a reincarnation of the devil. In ancient Rome, it was believed, that placing an owl feather on a person while they slept would enable you to discover their secrets. By invoking the power of the owl - some ancient people believed they would be able to see and hear what others intentionally tried to hide. Those without this ability would feel uncomfortable because they feared they would be unable to deceive, and their ulterior motives would be made clear. It was thought that those who worked with owl magic could see into the darkness of others' souls. The vision and hearing capabilities had metaphysical links to the gifts of clairvoyance (*"the ability to sense or receive psychic information through sight"*) and clairaudience (*"the ability to sense or receive psychic information through hearing"*).

Any ability/disability which is not understood or is misunderstood causes difficulty and division. It is safer to be '*the same*' and merge in. Standing out from the crowd and being different can carry a hefty price tag. History has shown how having a different opinion, religion, background, nationality, culture or simply trying to introduce a new concept, can be met with fear, which in turn can lead to hatred. And yet we are all unique.

Some of us are simply more sensory than others with one or more of our senses - smell, taste, sight, hearing, and touch being more acute. Some will have a stronger '*gut*' intuition or sense of how others are feeling. Others will be aware of information without being told. Once these simple facts are embraced, those who are highly sensitive can be acknowledged and assisted to fully participate in society. Their heightened senses accepted as a positive instead of a negative. Even if each person's uniqueness and emotional capacity is not understood but that it be at least accepted: then the positive impact these empowered and confident people have, as they take their rightful place in society, would have immeasurable benefits worldwide. It is time for society to champion these children, accept them and see their sensitivity as a characteristic to be celebrated. It is time to unlock the mystery of the sensitive child.

Being different can be difficult.
Everyone is different!
Not being perfect is difficult.
We are all perfectly imperfect!
Being sensitive does not have to be so difficult.
It simply requires openness, tolerance and
understanding.

NOTES

🕊

NOTES

NOTES

NOTES

NOTES

NOTES

NOTES